COMPUTING MADE SIMPLE

WORD 2000 MADE SIMPLE

PHOTOSHOP 5 MADE SIMPLE

WINDOWS 98 MADE SIMPLE

P K McBRIDE
THE INTERNET MADE SIMPLE
FULL COLOUR EDITION

These books explain the basics of software packages and computer topics in a clear and simple manner, providing just enough information to get started. They are ideal for users who want an insight into software packages and computers without being overwhelmed by technical jargon

- Easy to Follow
- Task Based
- Jargon Free
- Easy Steps
- Practical
- Excellent Value

MADE SIMPLE BOOKS
An imprint of Butterworth-Heinemann
http://www.bh.com

forget to visit our website http://www.madesimple.co.uk

NEW
AOL 4.0
Keith Brindley
0 7506 4626 8   1999

NEW
Access 2000
Moira Stephen
0 7506 4182 7   1999

NEW
Access 2000 in Business
Moira Stephen   1999
7506 4611 X   £11.99

Access 97 for Windows
Moira Stephen
0 7506 3800 1   1997

Access for Windows 95 (V.7)
Moira Stephen
0 7506 2818 9   1996

Access for Windows 3.1 (V.2)
Moira Stephen
0 7506 2309 8   1995

NEW
Adobe Acrobat & PDF
Graham Douglas
0 7506 4220 3   1999

NEW
Compuserve 2000
Keith Brindley
0 7506 4524 5   1999

Compuserve (V.3)
Keith Brindley
0 7506 3512 6   1998

NEW
Designing Internet Home Pages *Second Edition*
Lilian Hobbs
0 7506 4476 1   1999

NEW
Excel 2000
Stephen Morris
0 7506 4180 0   1999

NEW
Excel 2000 in Business
Stephen Morris   1999
0 7506 4609 8   £11.99

Excel 97 for Windows
Stephen Morris
0 7506 3802 8   1997

Excel for Windows 95 (V.7)
Stephen Morris
0 7506 2816 2   1996

Excel for Windows 3.1 (V.5)
Stephen Morris
0 7506 2070 6   1994

NEW
Explorer 5.0
P K McBride
0 7506 4627 6   1999

Explorer 4.0
Sam Kennington
0 7506 3796 X   1998

Explorer 3.0
Sam Kennington
0 7506 3513 4   1997

NEW
Internet In Co
P K McBride
0 7506 4576 8   £14.99

NEW
Internet for Windows 98
P K McBride
0 7506 4563 6   1999

Internet for Windows 95
P K McBride
0 7506 3846 X   1997

NEW
FrontPage 2000
Nat McBride
0 7506 4598 9   1999

FrontPage 97
Nat McBride
0 7506 3941 5   1998

NEW
The iMac Made Simple
Keith Brindley
0 7506 4608 X   1999

Microsoft Money 99
Moira Stephen
0 7506 4305 6   1999

NEW
Publisher 2000
Moira Stephen
0 7506 4597 0   1999

Publisher 97
Moira Stephen
0 7506 3943 1   1998

MS-DOS
Ian Sinclair
0 7506 2069 2   1994

Multimedia for Windows 95
Simon Collin
0 7506 3397 2   1997

Netscape Communicator 4.0
Sam Kennington
0 7506 4040 5   1998

Netscape Navigator (V.3)
P K McBride
0 7506 3514 2   1997

NEW
Office 2000
P K McBride
0 7506 4179 7   1999

Office 97
P K McBride
0 7506 3798 6   1997

NEW
Outlook 2000
P K McBride
0 7506 4414 1   1999

NEW
Pagemaker (V.6.5)
Steve Heath
0 7506 4050 2   1999

NEW
Photoshop 5
Martin Evening
Rod Wynne-Powell
0 7506 4334 X   1999

Moira Stephen
0 7506 4177 0   1999

Powerpoint 97 for Windows
Moira Stephen
0 7506 3799 4   1997

Powerpoint for Windows 95 (V.7)
Moira Stephen
0 7506 2817 0   1996

NEW
Sage Accounts
P K McBride
0 7506 4413 3   1999

Searching the Internet
P K McBride
0 7506 3794 3   1998

Windows 98
P K McBride
0 7506 4039 1   1998

Windows 95
P K McBride
0 7506 2306 3   1995

Windows 3.1
P K McBride
0 7506 2072 2   1994

NEW
Windows CE
Craig Peacock
0 7506 4335 8   1999

Windows NT (V4.0)
Lilian Hobbs
0 7506 3511 8   1997

NEW
Word 2000
Keith Brindley
0 7506 4181 9   1999

NEW
Word 2000 in Business
Keith Brindley   1999
0 7506 4610 1   £11.99

Word 97 for Windows
Keith Brindley
0 7506 3801 X   1997

Word for Windows 95 (V.7)
Keith Brindley
0 7506 2815 4   1996

Word for Windows 3.1 (V.6)
Keith Brindley
0 7506 2071 4   1994

Word Pro (4.0) for Windows 3.1
Moira Stephen
0 7506 2626 7   1995

Works for Windows 95 (V.4)
P K McBride
0 7506 3396 4   1996

Works for Windows 3.1 (V.3)
P K McBride
0 7506 2065 X   1994

Includes New Titles for 1999

CW00591506

Windows® 98
Made Simple

P.K.McBride

MADE SIMPLE
BOOKS

Made Simple
An imprint of Butterworth-Heinemann
Linacre House, Jordan Hill, Oxford OX2 8DP
225 Wildwood Avenue, Woburn, MA 01801-2041
A division of Reed Educational and Professional Publishing Ltd

℞ A member of the Reed Elsevier plc group

OXFORD   AUCKLAND   BOSTON
JOHANNESBURG   MELBOURNE   NEW DELHI

First published 1998
Reprinted 1999 (twice)

TRADEMARKS/REGISTERED TRADEMARKS
Computer hardware and software brand names mentioned in this book are protected
by their respective trademarks and are acknowledged.

British Library Cataloguing in Publication Data
A catalogue record for this book is available from the British Library

ISBN 0 7506 4039 1

⚛ Typeset by P.K.McBride, Southampton
Archtype, Bash Casual, Cotswold and Gravity fonts from Advanced Graphics Ltd
Icons designed by Sarah Ward © 1994
Printed and bound in Great Britain

PLANT A TREE

British Trust for
Conservation Volunteers

FOR EVERY TITLE THAT WE PUBLISH, BUTTERWORTH-HEINEMANN
WILL PAY FOR BTCV TO PLANT AND CARE FOR A TREE.

Contents

Preface

Windows, in its various forms, is now established as the world's leading operating system for personal computers. Windows 98 should ensure that Microsoft's dominance continues well into the next millenium.

Windows 98 Made Simple has been written primarily for the new computer user. The book starts by looking at the basic concepts and techniques of working with Windows – making choices, using the Help system and managing the screen.

Chapters 4 and 5 will show you how to organise your disks, so that you can store files safely and efficiently – and find them when you want them. We return to disks in Chapter 9, where we'll look at how to keep them in good working order.

In Chapter 6 we step briefly away from the desktop into the wider world of the Internet. There is no space in this small book to do justice to this vast topic, but I hope that you will at least get a sense of its possibilities – then turn to *The Internet Made Simple* to find out more!

One of the attractive features of Windows is that it lets you customise your system to suit the way that you work. In Chapters 7 and 8 you will see how to do this. The final chapter shows how to set up printers, and has a quick look at a few of the accessories.

I have aimed to give you enough to be able to start using Windows quickly and confidently. Once you have got into the Window's way of doing things, you will find it easy to extend your skills and knowledge.

P.K.McBride, 1998

Take note

Existing Windows 95 and 3.1 PCs can be upgraded to Windows 98 – providing that they have sufficient RAM memory and hard disk space. If you have upgraded from Windows 95, you will find few differences in this latest version. If you have upgraded from Windows 3.1, Windows 98 will come as a bit of a surprise, but as you get below the surface you will find that the two have much in common.

1 Start here

The Desktop

Windows is a Graphical User Interface (or **GUI**, pronounced *gooey*). What this means is that you work mainly by pointing at and clicking on symbols on the screen, rather than by typing commands. It is largely intuitive – i.e. the obvious thing to do is probably the right thing, and it is tolerant of mistakes. Many can be corrected as long as you tackle them straight away, and many others can be corrected easily, even after time has passed.

One of the ideas behind the design of Windows and of most Windows applications is that you should treat the screen as you would a desk. This is where you lay out your papers and books and tools to suit your own way of working. You may want to have more than one set of papers on the desktop at a time – so Windows lets you run several programs at once. You may want to have all your papers visible, for comparing or transferring data; you may want to concentrate on one, but have the others to hand. These – and other arrangements – are all possible.

Each program runs in its own window, and these can be arranged side by side, overlapping, or with the one you are working on filling the desktop and the others tucked out of the way, but still instantly accessible.

Just as there are many ways of arranging your desktop, so there are many ways of working with it – in fact, you are sometimes spoiled for choice!

It's your desktop. How you arrange it, and how you use it is up to you. This book will show you the simplest ways to use Windows 98 effectively.

❑ What you see on screen when you start Windows depends upon how the Desktop settings and shortcuts you are using.

❑ What the screen looks like once you are into your working session, is infinitely variable.

❑ Certain principles always apply and certain things are always there. It is the fact that all Windows applications share a common approach that makes Windows so easy to use.

Desktop – you can change the background pattern and the colours that are used.

Shortcuts – instant access to programs. You can create your own shortcuts.

Program windows – adjust their size and placing to suit yourself.

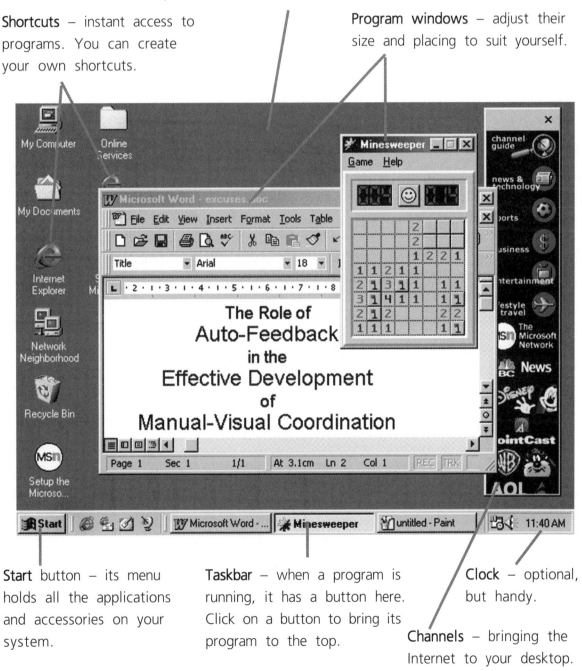

Start button – its menu holds all the applications and accessories on your system.

Taskbar – when a program is running, it has a button here. Click on a button to bring its program to the top.

Clock – optional, but handy.

Channels – bringing the Internet to your desktop.

Taming the mouse

You can't do much in Windows until you have tamed the mouse. It is used for locating the cursor, for selecting from menus, highlighting, moving and changing the size of objects, and much more. It won't bite, but it will wriggle until you have shown it who's in charge.

To control the mouse effectively you need a mouse mat or a thin pad of paper – mice don't run well on hard desktops.

The mouse and the cursor

Moving the mouse rolls the ball inside it. The ball turns the sensor rollers and these transmit the movement to the cursor. Straightforward? Yes, but note these points.

- If you are so close to the edge of the mat that you cannot move the cursor any further, pick up the mouse and plonk it back into the middle. If the ball doesn't move, the cursor doesn't move.

- You can set up the mouse so that when the mouse is moved faster, the cursor moves further. (See *Adjusting the mouse*, page 104.) Watch out for this when working on other people's machines.

Tip

A clean mouse is a happy mouse. If it starts to play up, take out the ball and clean it and the rollers with a damp tissue. Check for fluff build-up on the roller axles and remove any with tweezers.

Mouse actions

Point – move the cursor with your fingers **off** the buttons.

Click the left button to select a file, menu item or other object.

Click the right button to open a menu of commands that apply to that object.

Double click to run programs. You can set the gap between clicks to suit yourself. (See *Adjusting the mouse*, page 106.)

Drag – keep the left button down while moving the mouse. Used for resizing, drawing and similar jobs.

Drag and drop – drag an object and release the left button when it is in the right place. Used for moving objects.

The keyboard

Key guide

[Esc] – to Escape from trouble. Use it to cancel bad choices.

[Tab] – move between objects on screen.

[Caps Lock] – only put this on when you want to type a lot of capitals. The **Caps Lock** light shows if it is on.

[Shift] – use it for capitals and the symbols on the number keys.

[Ctrl] – often used with other keys to give keystroke alternatives to mouse commands.

[▓] – same as clicking [▓ Start] on the screen.

[Alt] – used, like [Ctrl], with other keys.

[Backspace] – rubs out the character to the left of the text cursor.

[Enter] – used at the end of a piece of text or to start an operation.

[Delete] – deletes files, folders and screen objects. Use with care.

Most Windows 98 operations can be handled quite happily by the mouse alone, leaving the keyboard for data entry. However, keys are necessary for some jobs, and if you prefer typing to mousing, it is possible to do most jobs from the keyboard. The relevant ones are shown here.

The function keys

Many operations can be run from these – if you can be bothered to learn the keystrokes. The only one really worth remembering is **[F1]**. This will always call up Help.

The control sets

The **Arrow** keys can often be used instead of the mouse for moving the cursor. Above them are more movement keys, which will let you jump around in text. **[Insert]** and **[Delete]** are also here.

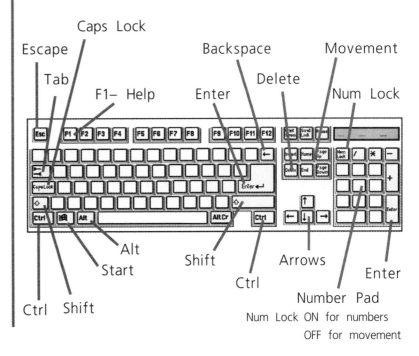

Num Lock ON for numbers
OFF for movement

5

Making choices

There are many situations where you have to specify a filename or an option. Sometimes you have to type in what you want, but in most cases, it only takes a click of the mouse or a couple of keystrokes.

Click or press [Alt]-[V]

Menus

To pull one down from the menu bar click on it, or press **[Alt]** and the underlined letter – usually the initial.

To select an item from a menu, click on it or type its underlined letter.

Some items are *toggles*. Selecting them turns an option on or off. ▤ beside the name shows that the option is on.

Point to open Sub-menu

▶ after an item shows that another menu leads from it.

Toggle

If you select an item with three dots ... after it, a dialog box will open to get more information from you.

Dialog box will follow

Click to get to its panel

Dialog boxes

These vary, but will usually have:

- **OK** to click when you have set the options, selected the file or whatever;

- **Apply** fix the options selected so far, but not leave the box;

- **Cancel** in case you decide the whole thing was a mistake;

- **Help** or **?** to get help on items in the box.

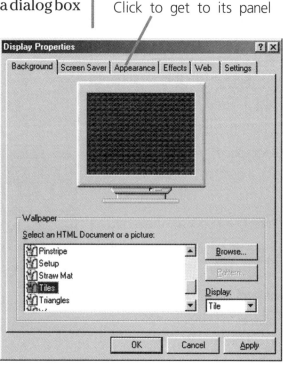

Tabs and panels

Some dialog boxes have several sets of options in them, each on a separate panel. These are identified by tabs at the top. Click on a tab to bring its panel to the front. Usually clicking [OK] on any panel will close the whole box. Use [Apply] when you have finished with one panel but want to explore others before closing.

Check boxes

These are used where there are several options, and you can use as many as you like at the same time.

📑 in the box shows that the option has been selected.

If the box is grey and the caption faint, the option is not available for the selected item.

Radio buttons

These are used for either/or options. Only one of the set can be selected.

The selected option is shown by black blob in the middle.

Drop-down lists

If a slot has a down arrow button on its right, click the button to drop down a list.

Click on an item in the list to select.

Take note

Most menus drop down from the top bar. The Start menu (next page) is different — it pops up.

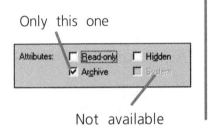

Only this one

Not available

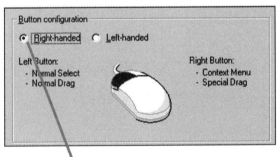

This one please

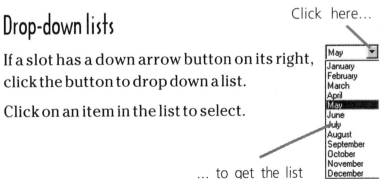

Click here...

... to get the list

Context menus

If you click the right button on anything on screen in Windows 98, a short menu will open beside it. This contains a set of commands and options that can be applied to the object.

What is on the menu depends upon the type of object and its *context*—hence the name. Two are shown here to give an idea of the possibilities.

Properties

Most menus have a **Properties** item. The contents of its dialog box also vary according to the nature of the object. For shortcuts, like the one for the Phone Dialer shown below, there is a *Shortcut* panel that controls the link to the program. The (hidden) *General* panel has a description of the file—this panel is in every file's Properties box.

Files can be Opened, Sent to a removable disk or off in the mail, and Deleted – amongst other things.

The **Clock** can be adjusted, and as it is on the Taskbar, you can also arrange the screen display from this menu.

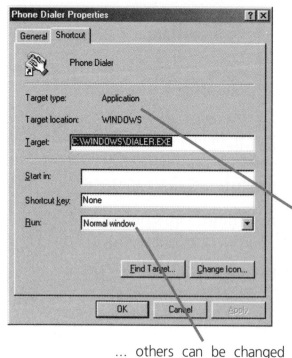

Some properties are there for information only ...

... others can be changed

8

Take note

Windows uses the word **DOCUMENT** to refer to any file that is created by an application. A word-processed report is obviously a document, but so is a picture file from a graphics package, data files from spreadsheets, video clips, sound files — in fact any file produced by any program.

Clicking on  at the bottom left of the screen, takes you into the menu system from which you can run applications, get help, find files, customize your system and close down at the end of a session.

The first level menu has 9 options:

Windows Update will connect you to Microsoft's site to download any new versions of the Windows files.

Programs is the main route to your applications. Leading from this is a second level of program folders, and selecting from there takes you to the icons for the programs in each folder.

Favorites holds links to selected places on the Internet (see page 78).

Documents holds a list of recently used document files. Selecting one from this list will run the relevant application and open the file for you to work on (see page 10).

Settings is used to customize the desktop and other aspects of the system (Chapter 8), set up printers (Chapter 10) and even rewrite the menu (Chapter 7).

Find will track down files and folders on your computer, your network and the Internet, and people on the Internet.

Help is one way into the Help system (Chapter 2).

Run lets you run a named application or starts up work on a document. This is mainly used for running DOS programs.

Shut down is the only safe way to end a session.

9

Running a program

The programs already on your PC, and most of those that you install later, will have an entry in the **Programs** menu. (The exceptions are mainly old MS-DOS programs.) Selecting one from here will run the program, ready for you to start work.

A program can also be run by selecting a document that was created by it. Those documents used most recently are stored in the **Documents** menu.

Basic steps

❑ **Running a program**

1 Click ▣Start.

2 Point to **Programs**.

3 Point to the folder that contains the program – you may have to point to the next menu level.

4 Click on the name to run the program.

❑ **From Documents**

5 Click ▣Start.

6 Point to **Documents**

7 Click on the file to get started on it.

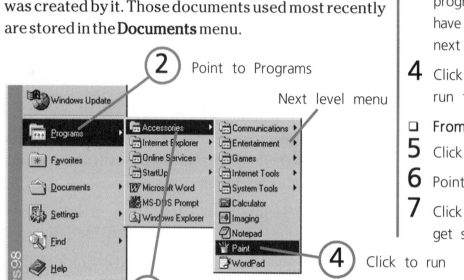

② Point to Programs

Next level menu

④ Click to run

③ Point to the folder

① Click Start

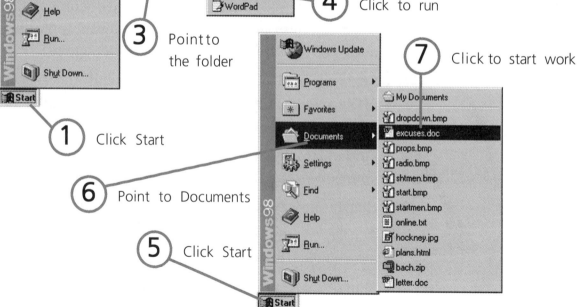

⑦ Click to start work

⑥ Point to Documents

⑤ Click Start

Basic steps

1 Click .

2 Click **Shut Down**.

3 If you want to restart, set the option.

4 Click **OK** .

When you have finished work on your computer, you must shut it down properly, and not just turn it off. This is essential. During your work session, application programs and Windows 98 itself may have created temporary work files – and data files that you have been editing may still be open in a memory buffer and not yet written safely to disk. An organised shut down closes and stores open files and clears away unwanted ones.

Restart

Sometimes you will find that a bug in an application or in Windows 98 has made the system hang or otherwise misbehave. Press **[Ctrl]-[Alt]-[Delete]** together to close that application, then shut down and restart. That generally clears most problems.

Take note

The Restart in MS-DOS mode is there mainly so that you can run old MS-DOS software that will not run within Windows – most can be run from the MS-DOS Prompt. You may well never use this Shut Down option.

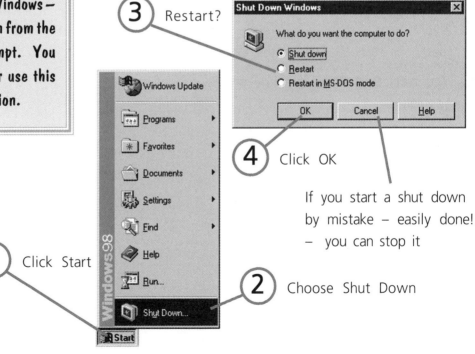

③ Restart?

④ Click OK

If you start a shut down by mistake – easily done! – you can stop it

① Click Start

② Choose Shut Down

Summary

- ❑ Windows is an **intuitive** system – if something *feels* right, it probably *is* right.

- ❑ All Windows software works in much the same way, so once you have got the hang of one program, you are half way to learning the next.

- ❑ The **mouse** is an important tool. Practise using it – a good excuse for playing the games!

- ❑ Some operations are easier with **keys**, and just a few can only be done from the keyboard.

- ❑ **Selections** can usually be made by picking from a list or clicking on a button or check box.

- ❑ Every object has a **context menu** containing those commands that you may want to use with it.

- ❑ The **Start** button is the main way into the system. Get to know your way around its menus.

- ❑ Applications can be run directly from the **Programs** menu, or through files in the **Documents** list.

- ❑ You must **Shut Down** properly at the end of a session.

2 Help!

The Help system

The Help system is the same for all new Windows 98 software, but is slightly different in older Windows 95 and 3.1 applications. You can get help in several ways:

- The main Help system, run from the Start menu;

- Help on applications and accessories, run from their menus;

- Query help on dialog boxes.

In all Help systems there are three approaches:

- an organised **Contents** list;

- **Index**ed Help pages;

- a word-based **Search** facility.

Basic steps

- From the Desktop

1 Click **Start**.

2 Click on **Help**.

- From an application

3 Click on **Help** on the menu bar.

4 Select **Help Topics** – Windows 98 programs.

or

5 Select **Help Contents** – Windows 95 or 3.1.

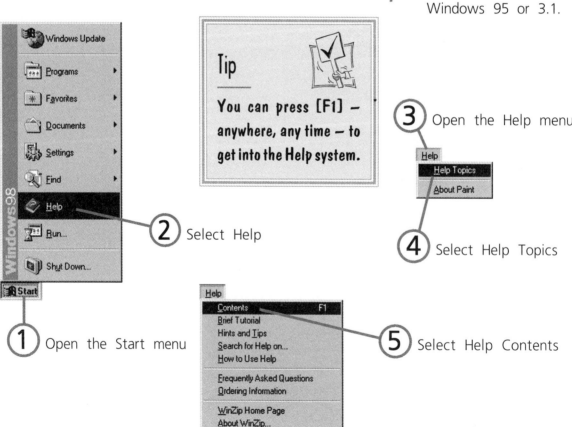

Tip

You can press [F1] – anywhere, any time – to get into the Help system.

① Open the Start menu

② Select Help

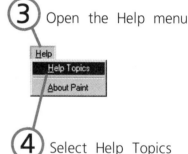

③ Open the Help menu

Help
Help Topics
About Paint

④ Select Help Topics

Help
Contents   F1
Brief Tutorial
Hints and Tips
Search for Help on...
How to Use Help
Frequently Asked Questions
Ordering Information
WinZip Home Page
About WinZip...

⑤ Select Help Contents

Basic steps

1 Click the **Contents** tab if this panel is not at the front already.

2 Click on a 📘 icon or its text to see the page titles – or the next level of books.

3 Click on a [?] icon or its text to read a page.

4 Click on <u>Related Topics</u> to reach any linked pages

5 Click [✕] to exit Help.

The Toolbar

Hide Closes the Tabs (the left of the window) and is replaced by **Show** to reopen it.

Back Return to previous Help page.

Forward On to next (visited) Help page.

Options For keyboard control – can be opened by [Alt]–[O].

Web Help Link to Microsoft Web site.

Contents

This approach treats the Help pages as a book. You scan through the headings to find a section that seems to cover what you want, and open that to see the page titles. (Some sections have sub-sections, making it a two or three-stage process to get to page titles.)

Some Help pages have <u>Related topics</u> links to take you on to further pages.

① Use the Contents panel

② Open a book

⑤ Exit Help

③ Open a page

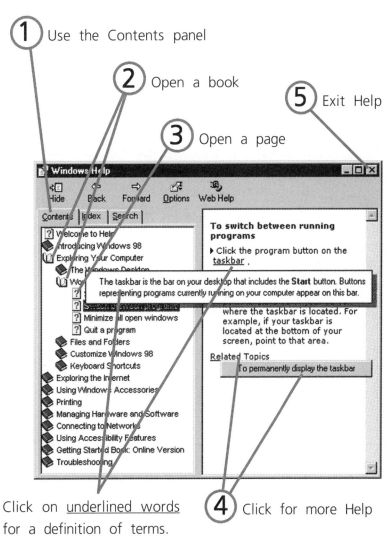

Click on <u>underlined words</u> for a definition of terms.

④ Click for more Help

Using the Index

Though the Contents are good for getting an overview of how things work, if you want help on a specific problem – usually the case – you are better off with the Index.

This is organised through an cross-referenced list of terms. The main list is alphabetical, with sub-entries, just like the index in a book. And, as with an index in a book, you can plough through it slowly from the top, or skip through to find the words that start with the right letters. Once you find a suitable entry, you can display the list of cross-referenced topics and pick one of those.

1 Click the **Index** tab.

2 Start to type a word into the slot then scroll to the topic.

3 Select an Index entry.

4 Click Display .

5 Pick a topic from the **Topics Found** list.

6 Click Display .

❑ If there is only one relevant topic page, the system will take you directly to it after Step 4.

(1) Open the Index panel

(2) Start to type

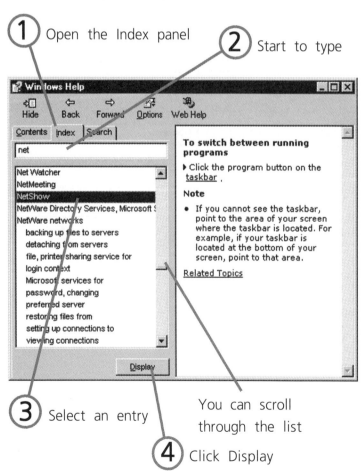

(3) Select an entry

You can scroll through the list

(4) Click Display

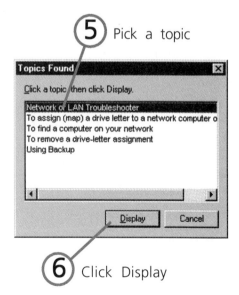

(5) Pick a topic

(6) Click Display

Basic steps

1 Click the **Search** tab.

2 Type a keyword into the slot.

3 Click [List Topics].

4 If you get too many topics, type a second word to narrow the search and click [List Topics] again.

5 Pick a topic from the list.

6 Click [Display].

On the Index panel you are hunting through the titles of Help pages. On the Search panel, the system looks for matching *keywords* within pages.

● A keyword can be any word which might occur in the pages that you are looking for.

● If you give two or more, the system will only list pages which contain all those words.

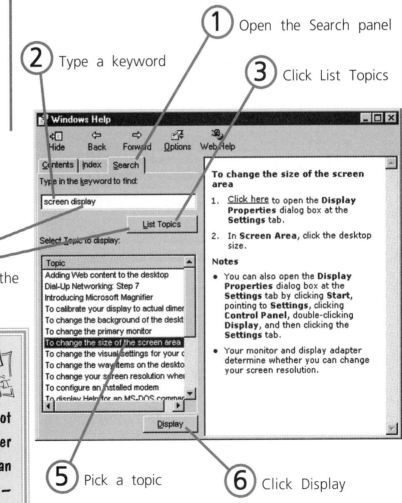

① Open the Search panel

② Type a keyword

③ Click List Topics

④ Narrow the search?

⑤ Pick a topic

⑥ Click Display

Tip

Sometimes the screen is not redrawn properly after displaying the definition of an underlined term. Use Options – Refresh to restore the display.

Finding Help

In older Windows 95 applications you will meet this in place of the Search panel. It is based on the same principles – searching for matching words within Help pages – but is used in a slightly different way.

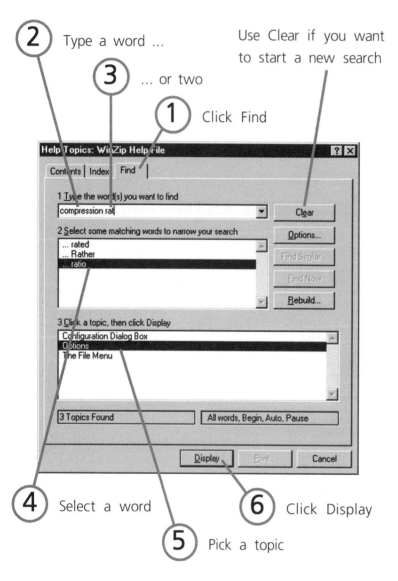

(2) Type a word ...

(3) ... or two

Use Clear if you want to start a new search

(1) Click Find

(4) Select a word

(5) Pick a topic

(6) Click Display

1 Open the **Find** panel.

2 Type your word into the top slot. As you type, words starting with the typed letters appear in the pane beneath.

3 If you want to narrow the search, go back to Step 2, type a space after your first word and give another.

4 Select the most suitable word from the **Narrow the search** pane.

5 Select a topic from the lower pane.

6 Click [Display].

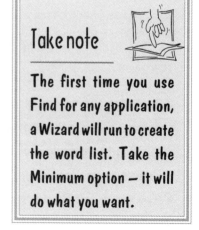

Take note

The first time you use **Find** for any application, a Wizard will run to create the word list. Take the **Minimum** option – it will do what you want.

Basic steps

1 On the **Find** panel, click [Options...].

2 Select **All the words...** where you are using several words to focus on one topic.

3 Select **At least one...** where you are giving alternatives, hoping that it recognises one.

4 Decide when you want the system to **Begin searching**.

5 Click [OK].

Find options

There are several Options that you can set to alter the nature of the search or narrow its scope.

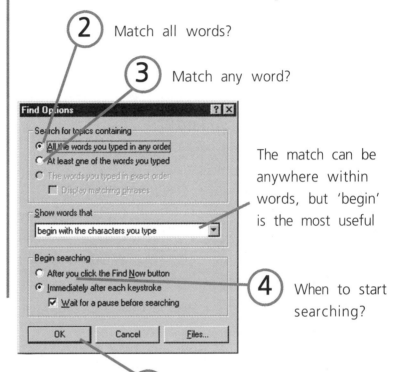

(2) Match all words?

(3) Match any word?

The match can be anywhere within words, but 'begin' is the most useful

(4) When to start searching?

(5) Click OK

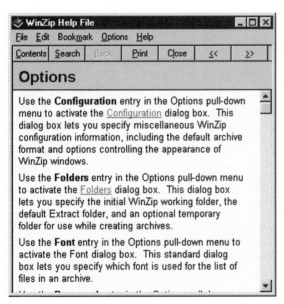

Older applications display Help pages in a separate window. WIth these, use **Contents** or **Search** to return to the main panel if you need more Help. The illustration comes from WinZip, a program that compresses and uncompresses files – an essential tool for anyone who intends to get material of the Internet. Find out more about it on the Web at http://www.winzip.com.

Instant Help

As well as the main Help system, Windows 98 offers a couple of other brief, but useful, forms of help.

The query icon

All dialog boxes and panels in Windows 98 and its components – and in any new or Windows 95 applications – have an ? icon on the top right of the status bar. You will also find an ? icon on the toolbar of some applications. They can both be used for finding out more about objects on screen.

Basic steps

1 Click on the ? or ? icon.

2 Click the ? cursor on the button, option or other item that you want to know about.

3 After you have read the Help box, click anywhere to close it.

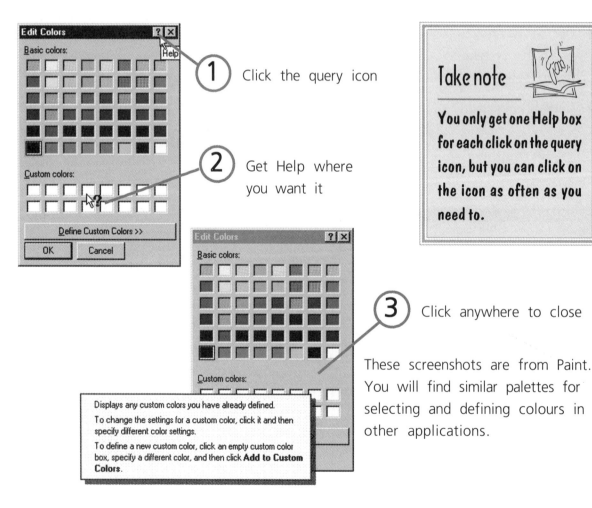

① Click the query icon

② Get Help where you want it

> ### Take note
>
> **You only get one Help box for each click on the query icon, but you can click on the icon as often as you need to.**

③ Click anywhere to close

These screenshots are from Paint. You will find similar palettes for selecting and defining colours in other applications.

Displays any custom colors you have already defined.

To change the settings for a custom color, click it and then specify different color settings.

To define a new custom color, click an empty custom color box, specify a different color, and then click **Add to Custom Colors**.

Help on icons

Icons are supposed to be self-explanatory, but their purpose cannot always be summed up in a small image. Never fear, help is near!

Let the cursor rest over an icon for a moment and a label will pop up to tell you what it is. If that isn't enough to tell you what it does, at least you have a name to look up in the Help Index.

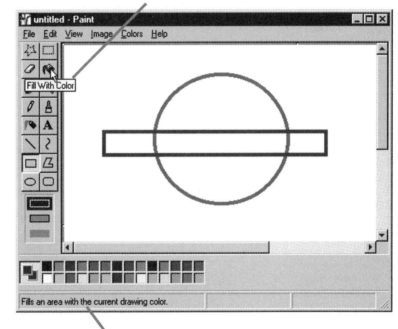

Tip

Even if the Help box doesn't give you enough information, it will give you the words you need to find more detailed Help. From the example on the right, we can get 'Fill', and using that in a Search gets us to detailed instructions on how to fill shapes with colour.

Take note

If a window is in Restore mode — i.e. smaller than the full screen (see page 26 for more) — the message area in the Status Bar may not be long enough to display the Help message in full.

Summary

❑ Help is always available.

❑ Use the **Contents** panel when you are browsing to see what topics are covered.

❑ Use the **Index** to go directly to the help on a specified operation or object.

❑ If you can't locate the Help in the Index, use the **Search** (Windows 98) or **Find** (older Windows applications) facility to track down the pages.

❑ For Help with items in a **dialog box** or **panel**, click the query icon and point to the item.

❑ If you hold the cursor over an **icon**, a brief prompt will pop up to tell you what it does. There will also be a Help message in the Status Bar.

3 Window control

The window frame

This is more than just a pretty border. It contains all the controls you need for adjusting the display.

Frame edge

This has a control system built into it. When a window is in Restore mode – i.e. smaller than full-screen – you can drag on the edge to make it larger or smaller. (See *Changing the size*, page 31.)

Title bar

This is to remind you of where you are and is also used for moving the window. Drag on this and the window moves. (See *Moving windows*, page 30.)

Maximize, Minimize and Restore

These buttons change the display mode. Only one of Maximize and Restore will be visible at any one time. (See *Window modes*, page 26.)

Close

One of several ways to close a window and the program that was running in it. (See *Closing windows*, page 33.)

Control menu icon

There is no set image for this icon, as every application has its own, but clicking on whatever is here will open the Control menu. This can be used for changing the screen mode or closing the window. (See *Window modes*, page 26.) Double-clicking this icon will close down the window.

Take note

Most applications can handle several documents at once, each in its own window. These are used in almost the same way as program windows. The applications usually have a **Window** menu containing controls for the document windows.

24

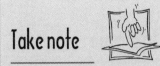
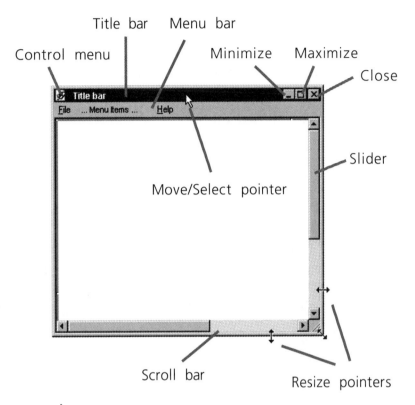

Menu bar

Immediately below the Title bar in an application's window is a bar containing the names of its menus. Clicking on one of these will drop down a list of commands.

Scroll bars

These are present on the right side and bottom of the frame if the display contained by the window is too big to fit within it. The **Sliders** in the Scroll Bars show you where your view is, relative to the overall display. Moving these allows you to view a different part of the display. (See *Scrolling*, page 32.)

Window modes

All programs are displayed on screen in windows, and these can normally have three modes:

- Maximized – filling the whole screen;
- Minimized – not displayed, though still present as a button on the Task bar;
- Restore – adjustable in size and in position.

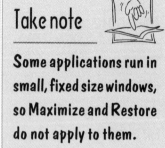

Take note

Some applications run in small, fixed size windows, so Maximize and Restore do not apply to them.

· Maximized

In **Restore** mode

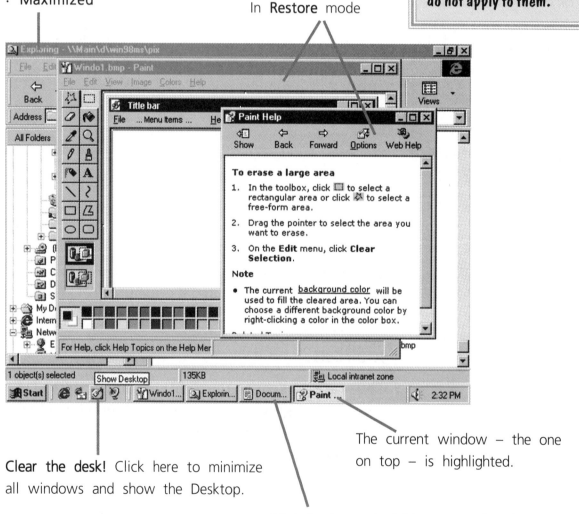

Clear the desk! Click here to minimize all windows and show the Desktop.

The current window – the one on top – is highlighted.

Minimized – not visible except for this.

Basic steps

Changing display modes

Clicking on the buttons in the top right corner of the frame is the simplest way to switch between **Maximize** and **Restore** modes, and to **Minimize** a window. If you prefer it can be done using the Control Menu.

☐ To make a window full-screen

Click ▣ or select **Maximize** from the Control Menu

☐ To restore a window to variable size

Click ▣ or select **Restore** from the Control Menu

☐ To shrink a window to an icon

Click ▣ or select **Minimize** from the Control Menu

The Control menu

Click the icon at the top left to open this. Options that they don't apply at the time will be 'greyed out'. The menu here came from a variable size window. One from a full-screen window would have **Move, Size** and **Maximize** in grey.

Using the Taskbar

Click a program's button to bring its window to the top. Right click the button to open the Control menu.

Left-click to activate

Right-click for the menu

Keyboard control

[Alt]–[Space] opens the Control menu of an application.

[Alt]–[-] (minus) opens the Control menu of a document.

Minimized documents

When you minimize a document window, within an application, it shrinks to a tiny title bar, with just enough room for a name and the icons. Click Maximize or Restore to open it out again.

Restore   Maximize

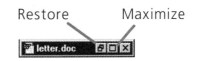

Arranging windows

If you want to have two or more windows visible at the same time, you will have to arrange them on your desktop. There are Windows tools that will do it for you, or you can do it yourself.

If you right-click the Taskbar, its menu has options to arrange the windows on the desktop. Open it and you will see **Cascade**, **Tile Vertical** and **Tile Horizontal**. Similar options are on the Window menu of most applications, though these only affect the layout *within* the programs.

Cascade places the windows overlapping with just the title bars of the back ones showing. You might just as well Maximize the current window, and use the Taskbar buttons to get to the rest.

Either of the Tile layouts can be the basis of a well-arranged desktop.

1 Maximize or **Restore** the windows that you want to include in the layout. **Minimize** those that you will not be using actively.

2 Right-click the **Taskbar** to open its menu

3 Select **Tile Horizontal** or **Tile Vertical**.

4 If you only want to work in one window at a time, **Maximize** it, and **Restore** it back into the arrangement when you have done.

Tip

If you want to adjust the balance of the layout, you can move and resize the windows.

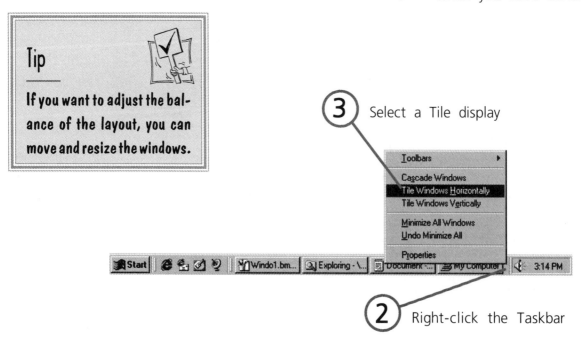

③ Select a Tile display

Toolbars

Cascade Windows
Tile Windows Horizontally
Tile Windows Vertically

Minimize All Windows
Undo Minimize All

Properties

Start Windo1.bm... | Exploring - \... | Document -... | My Computer | 3:14 PM

② Right-click the Taskbar

Tile

Tile arranges open windows side by side (Vertical), or in rows (Horizontal) – with more than three windows, the tiling is in both directions. As the window frames take up space, the actual working area is significantly reduced. Obviously, larger, high-resolution screens are better for multi-window work, but even on a 1024 x 768 display you cannot do much serious typing in a tiled window.

Tip

Cascade displays work better than Tile displays on small screens.

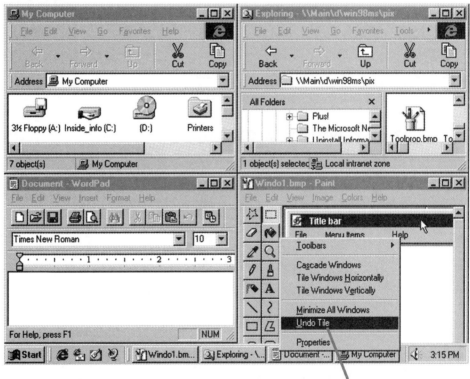

The Taskbar menu now has an Undo Tile option to restore your screen to its previous state.

Tip

It is generally simplest to work with the active window Maximized and any others Minimized out of the way.

Moving windows

When a window is in **Restore** mode – open but not full screen – it can be moved anywhere on the screen.

- If you are not careful it can be moved almost off the screen! Fortunately, at least a bit of the title bar will still be visible, and that is the handle you need to grab to pull it back into view.

Basic steps

1 If the Title Bar isn't highlighted, click on the window to make it the active one.

2 Point at the Title Bar and hold the left button down.

3 Drag the window to its new position – you will only see a grey outline moving.

4 Release the button.

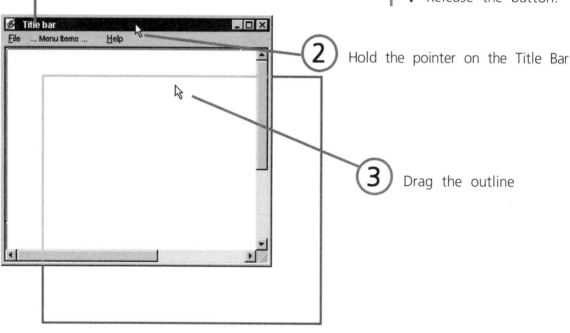

① Make the window active

② Hold the pointer on the Title Bar

③ Drag the outline

④ Release to drop into its new position

Changing the size

Basic steps

1 Move the pointer to the edge or corner that you want to pull in or out.

2 When you see the double-headed arrow, hold down the left mouse button and drag the outline to the required size.

3 Release the button.

When a window is in Restore mode, you can change its size and shape by dragging the edges of the frame to new positions.

Combined with the moving facility, this lets you arrange your desktop exactly the way you like it.

● The resize pointers only appear when the pointer is just on an edge, and they disappear again if you go too far. Practise! You'll soon get the knack of catching them.

You can drag any edge or corner

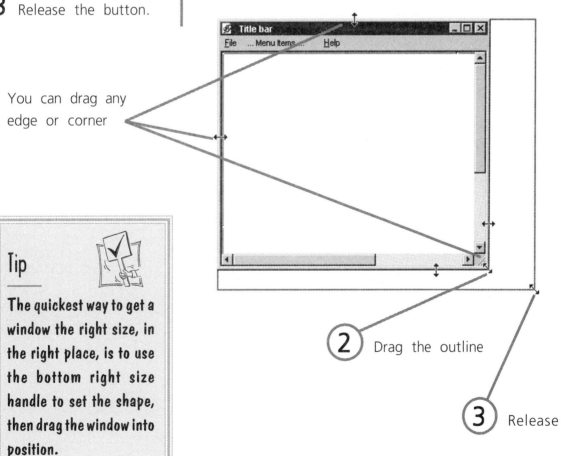

2 Drag the outline

3 Release

Tip

The quickest way to get a window the right size, in the right place, is to use the bottom right size handle to set the shape, then drag the window into position.

Scrolling

What you can see in a window is often only part of the story. The working area of the application may well be much larger. If there are scroll bars on the side and/or bottom of the window, this tells you that there is more material outside the frame. The scroll bars let you pull some of this material into view.

❑ Drag the **Slider** to scroll the view in the window. Keep your pointer moving straight along the bar or it won't work!

❑ Click an **Arrow** to edge the slider towards the arrow. Hold down for a slow continuous scroll.

❑ Click on the **Bar** beside the Slider to make it jump towards the pointer.

> ## Tip
>
> **If a window is blank — and you think there should be something there — push the sliders to the very top and left. That's where your work is likely to be.**

Sliders

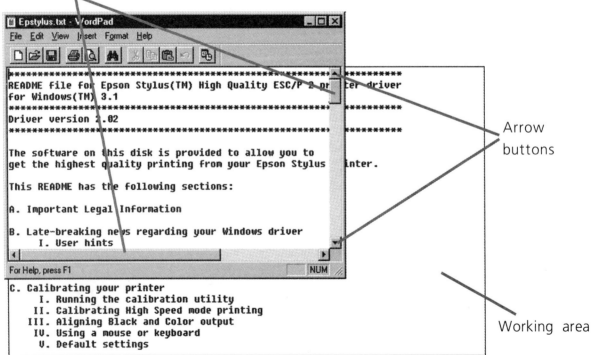

Arrow buttons

Working area

Basic steps

- ❏ Closing an active window

1 Click ▣ or press [Alt]-[F4].

- ❏ Closing from the Taskbar

2 Right-click the progam's button to get its menu.

3 Select **Close**.

4 If you have forgotten to save your work, take the opportunity that is offered to you.

Closing windows

When you close a window, you close down the program that was running inside it.

If you haven't saved your work, most programs will point this out and give you a chance to save before closing.

There are at least five different ways of closing. Here are the simplest three:

- ● If the window is in Maximized or Restore mode, click the close icon at the top right of the Title bar. (If your mouse control is not too good, you may well do this when you are trying to Maximize the window!)

- ● If the window has been Minimized onto the Taskbar, right-click on its button to open the Control menu and use **Close**.

- ● If you prefer working from keys, press [**Alt**]-[**F4**].

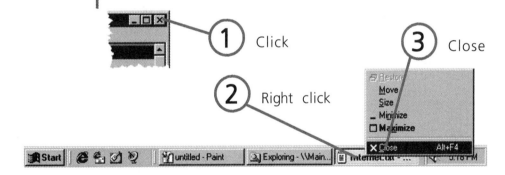

① Click ③ Close

② Right click

Tip

When you have finished with a program, close it. Even Minimized windows use some memory and slow down performance.

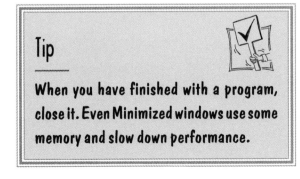

④ Save it?

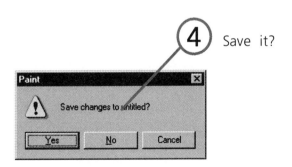

Summary

❑ You can move between windows by clicking on any visible part of them – though the active parts of the frame should be avoided.

❑ Windows can be displayed in **Maximized** (full-screen) or **Restore** (variable size) modes, or **Minimized** to icons.

❑ **Minimized windows** can be restored to full size by clicking on their icon in the Taskbar.

❑ Windows can be arranged on the desktop by picking **Cascade** or **Tile** from the **Taskbar** menu.

❑ A window can be **moved** about the screen by dragging on its title bar.

❑ You can change the **size** of a window (in Restore mode) by dragging on any of its edges.

❑ The **scroll bars** will let you move the working area inside a window.

❑ **Closing** a window closes its program.

4 Exploring folders

Explorer v. My Computer

Windows 98 gives you four tools for managing your files and folders.

Explorer (page 40)

This has a dual display, with the folder structure on the left and the contents of the current folder on the right.

Though Explorer will only display the contents of one folder, you can run two or more copies of it at once. This can be useful when you are moving or copying files from one part of the system to another.

Explorer can access the folders in all of the drives attached to your computer, and any that may be accessible to you over a network.

My Computer (page 50)

This has a simpler display than Explorer. It works in a single-pane window, and when first opened it gives an overview of the components of your own system. You can then open another window to get a detailed look at folders in a drive, and continue opening further windows to go deeper into folders.

Network Neighborhood

This is the same as My Computer, but opens with the focus on any networked machines.

Internet Explorer (Chapter 6)

Though originally designed for exploring the Internet, this can also be used for exploring your system or local network. My Computer and Network Neighborhood can both be opened and viewed through Internet Explorer.

Take note

Which software you use for your file management is up to you. I prefer Windows Explorer for most jobs — certainly for organising files and folders. When I'm simply looking to see what's where, I'll sometimes use My Computer or Network Neighborhood — or Internet Explorer if it happens to be running.

The jargon

- **Root** – the folder of the disk. All other folders branch off from the root.

- **Parent** – a folder that contains another.

- **Child** – a sub-folder of a Parent.

- **Branch** – the structure of sub-folders open off from a folder.

Tip

When planning the folder structure, keep it simple. Too many folders within folders can make it hard to find files.

If you are going to work successfully with Windows 98 – or any computer system – you must understand how its disk storage is organised, and how to manage files efficiently and safely. In this chapter, we will look at the filing system, working with folders and the screen displays of Explorer and My Computer. In later sections, we will cover managing files and looking after your disks.

Folders

The hard disks supplied on modern PCs are typically 2 gigabytes or larger. g Gigabyte is 1 billion bytes and each byte can hold one character (or part of a number or graphic). That means that a typical hard disk can hold up to 300 million words – enough for 1,500 hefty novels! More to the point, if you were using it to store letters and reports, it could hold many thousands of them. It must be organised if you are ever to find your files.

Folders provide this organisation. They are containers in which related files can be placed to keep them together, and away from other files. A folder can also contain sub-folders – which can themselves by subdivided. You can think of the first level of folders as being sets of filing cabinets; the second level are drawers within the cabinets, and the next level divisions within the drawers. (And these could have subdividers – there is no limit to this.)

Don't just store all your files in My Documents – it will get terribly crowded! Have a separate folder for each type of file, or each area of work (or each user of the computer), subdividing as necessary, so that no folder holds more than a few dozen files.

Paths

The structure of folders is often referred to as the **tree**. It starts at the **root**, which is the drive letter – C: for your main hard disk – and branches off from there.

A folder's position in the tree is described by its **path**. For most operations, you can identify a folder by clicking on it in a screen display, but now and then you will have to type its path. This should start at the drive letter and the root, and include every folder along the branch, with a backslash (\) between the names.

For example:

C:\DTP

C:\WORDPROC\LETTERS

When you want to know a path, look it up in the Explorer display and trace the branches down from the root.

Filenames

A filename has two parts – the name and an extension.

The **name** can be as long as you like, and include almost any characters – including spaces. But don't let the freedom go to your head. The longer the name, the greater the opportunity for typing errors. The most important thing to remember when naming a file is that the name must mean something to you, so that you can find it easily next time you come back to the job.

The **extension** can be from 0 to 3 characters, and is separated from the rest of the name by a dot. It is used to identify the nature of the file. Windows and MS-DOS use the extensions COM, EXE, SYS, INI, DLL to identify special files of their own.

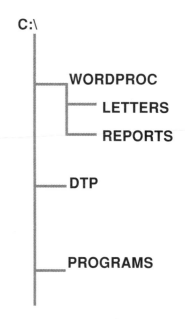

```
C:\
    ┌── WORDPROC
    │       ├── LETTERS
    │       └── REPORTS
    ├── DTP
    └── PROGRAMS
```

Take note

Whatever you call a file, Windows 98 will also give it a name in the **MS-DOS** format – which limits the main part to 8 letters – for use with older applications. The name will start with the same six letters, then have ~ (tilde) and a number, e.g. 'LETTER TO BILL.DOC' becomes 'LETTER~1.DOC'

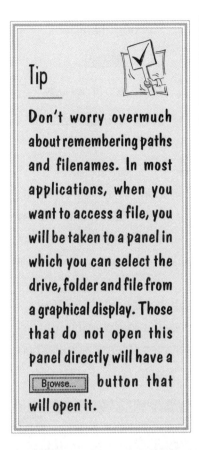
Most applications also use their own special extensions. Word-processor files are often marked with DOC or TXT; spreadsheet files are usually XLS or WK1; databases files typically have DB extensions.

If you are saving a file in a word-processor, spreadsheet or other application, and are asked for a filename, you normally only have to give the first part. The application will take care of the extension. If you do need to give an extension, make it meaningful. BAK is a good extension for backup files; TXT for text files.

When an application asks you for a filename – and the file is in the *current* folder – type in the name and extension only. If the file is in *another* folder, type in the path, a backslash separator and then the filename.

For example:

MYFILE.DOC

C:\WORPROC\REPORTS\MAY25.TXT

A:\MYFILE.BAK

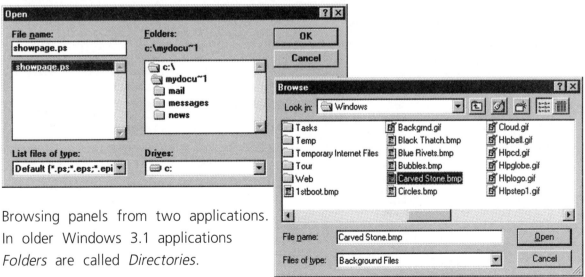

Browsing panels from two applications. In older Windows 3.1 applications *Folders* are called *Directories*.

Windows Explorer

Basic steps

☐ Starting Explorer

1 Click **⊞Start**.

2 Point to **Programs**.

3 Click **Windows Explorer**.

4 Click on a folder's icon 📁 or its name to open 📂 it and display its Contents.

In the Explorer window, the main working area is split, with *All Folders* on the left, in the Explorer Bar, and the *Contents* on the right.

The **All Folders** panel may show the disk drives and first level of folders only, but folders can be expanded to show the sub-folders. (See *Expanding folders*, page 44.)

The **Contents** shows the files and sub-folders in the currently selected folder. These can be displayed as large or small icons accompanied by the name only, or with details of the file's size, type and date it was last modified. (See *Arranging icons*, page 54.) The overall display can be as a Web page (below), or in the Classic style (opposite).

The **Status Bar** shows the number of files in the folder, on the right, and the size of the selected files, on the left.

When viewed as a Web page, a description of the selected file is shown here

Click to close the Explorer Bar

Contents

Explorer Bar, displaying All Folders

Drives

Root

First level folder

Current folder

Sub-folder

Status Bar

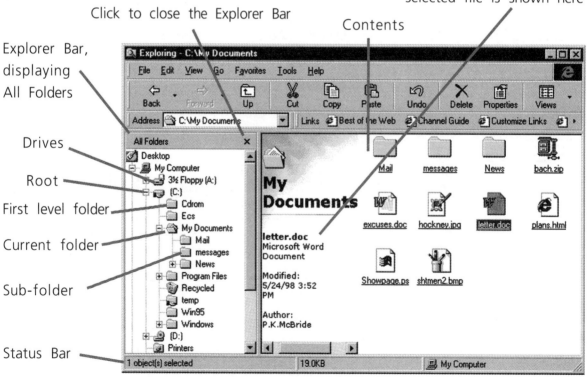

40

Basic steps

View options

□ **Displaying Toolbars**

1 Open the **View** menu.

2 Point to **Toolbars** then click on a toolbar to turn it on or off.

□ **Web page view**

3 Open the **View** menu.

4 Click **As Web Page** to turn the style on or off.

□ **Icons and lists**

5 Open the **View** menu.

or

6 Click ![Views].

7 Choose a display style.

The display options can be set from the View menu and the Views button. These options can be set at any time.

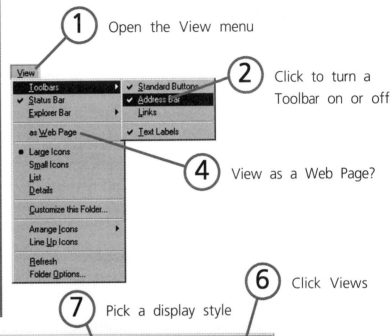

① Open the View menu

② Click to turn a Toolbar on or off

④ View as a Web Page?

⑥ Click Views

⑦ Pick a display style

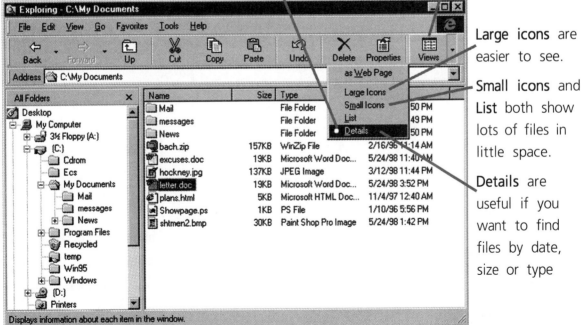

Large icons are easier to see.

Small icons and **List** both show lots of files in little space.

Details are useful if you want to find files by date, size or type

Folder Options

The **General** options control the basic nature of folder displays – not just in Explorer, but also in My Computer and Network Neighborhood. You can set folders to behave like Web pages, with links to files and folders underlined and responding to a single click, or have the 'classic' displays, where you click once to select and double-click to activate. A combination of the two is also possible.

Hidden files

The **View** panel controls the display of files. Here the key question is whether to show 'hidden' and system files. These are ones that you do not usually need to see and which are safer out of the way.

- **Application extensions** – files with **.DLL** extensions. They are parts of larger programs, cannot be used by themselves and must not be deleted.

- **System files** – marked by **.SYS** after the name. These are essential to Windows 98's internal workings.

- **Drivers** – with **.VXD** or **.DRV** extensions. These make printers, screens and other hardware work properly.

The *Windows* and *Windows/System* folders are full of these.

Basic steps

1 Open the **View** menu.

2 Select **Folder Options**.

3 On the **General** panel select **Web style** or **Classic style**.

or

4 Select **Custom** and click [Settings...].

5 Set **View** and **Click** options as required.

6 Go to the **View** panel.

7 Click the text or box to turn options on or off – to test the effect click [Apply].

8 When you have done. click [Close].

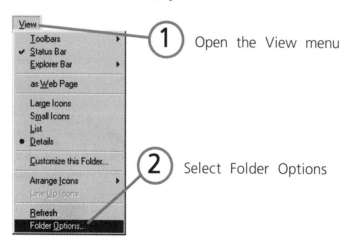

① Open the View menu

② Select Folder Options

Take note

You can also reach the Folder Options from My Computer and Network Neighborhood, or from the Settings on the Start menu.

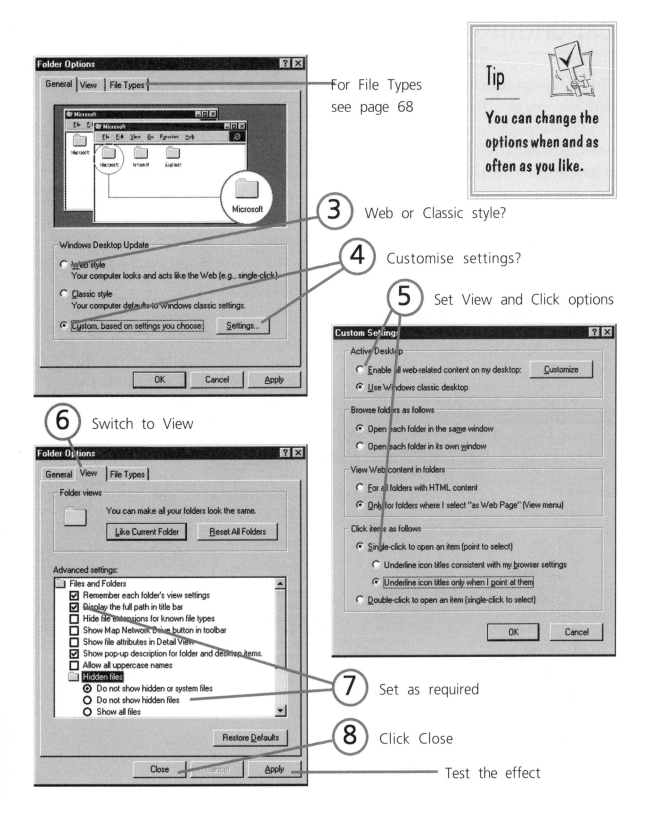

For File Types
see page 68

For File Types
see page 68

Tip

You can change the
options when and as
often as you like.

(3) Web or Classic style?

(4) Customise settings?

(5) Set View and Click options

(6) Switch to View

(7) Set as required

(8) Click Close

Test the effect

43

Expanding folders

The *All Folders* structure can be shown in outline form, or with some or all of its branches shown in full. The best display is always the simplest that will show you all you need. This usually means that most of the structure is collapsed back to its first level of main folders, with one or two branches expanded to show particular sub-folders. It is sometimes worth expanding the whole lot, just to get an idea of the overall structure and to see how sub-folders fit together.

If a folder has sub-folders, it will have a symbol beside it.

+ has sub-folders, and can be expanded

− sub-folders displayed and can be collapsed.

Basic steps

□ **To expand a folder**
1 Click **+** by its name.
2 Click **+** by any sub-folders if you want to fully expand the whole branching set.

□ **To collapse a folder**
3 Click **−** by its name.

□ **To collapse a whole branch**
4 Click **−** by the folder at the top of the branched set.

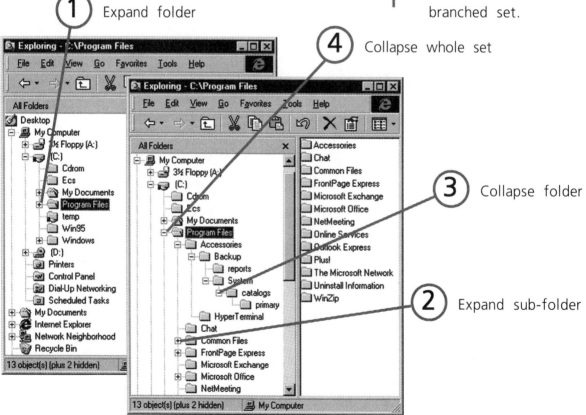

① Expand folder

④ Collapse whole set

③ Collapse folder

② Expand sub-folder

Basic steps

1 Point to the folder name and click the right mouse button.

2 Select **Properties** from the short menu.

3 Wait for for the system to work out the total space and number of files.

4 Click ☒ to close the Properties panel.

Folder properties

Expanding a folder will show you what is in it, but not how much space all its files and sub-folders occupy. The space report in the Status bar tells you how much is used by the files in the current folder only – not in its sub-folders. The total space figure can be important if you want to backup the folder, or copy it to floppies. The Properties panel will tell us this – and other things.

① Right click

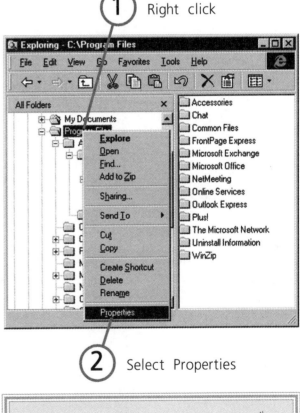

③ Check the totals

④ Close

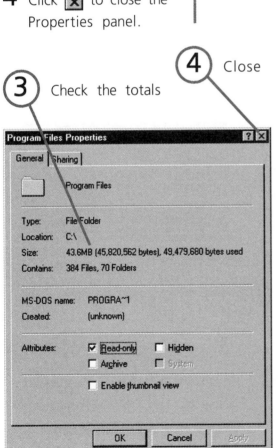

② Select Properties

Take note

You can right-click almost everything to see its Properties and find out more about the item.

Creating a folder

Organised people set up their folders before they need them, so that they have places to store their letters – private and business, reports, memos, notes, and whatever, when they start to write them on their new system. They have a clear idea of the structure that they want, and create their folders at the right branches.

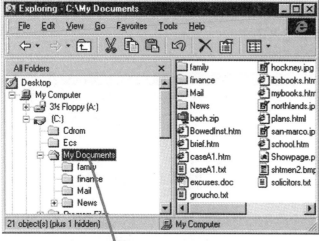

① Click on the parent

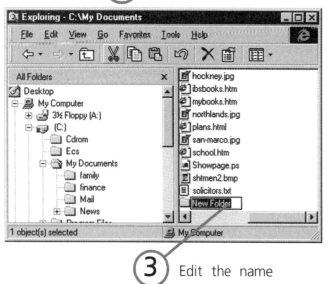

③ Edit the name

Basic steps

1 Select the folder that will be the parent of your new one, or the root if you want a new first-level folder.

2 Open the **File** menu and point to **New** then select **Folder**.

3 Replace 'New Folder' with a new name – any length, any characters as with filenames.

② Select File – New – Folder

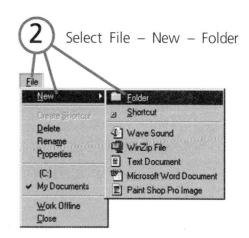

Tip

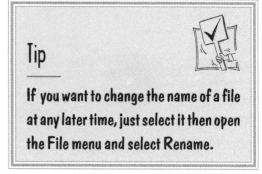

If you want to change the name of a file at any later time, just select it then open the File menu and select Rename.

46

Your folder structure

How you organise your folders is entirely up to you, but these guidelines may help.

If several people use the same computer, they should each have their own folders – which may be sub-divided to match their interests.

Don't have too many levels of sub-folders – it can get confusing. Create your main folders at the C: drive or in My Documents, and aim for a maximum of two levels of sub-folders within these.

It's a pain having to work down through four or five levels to reach stuff!

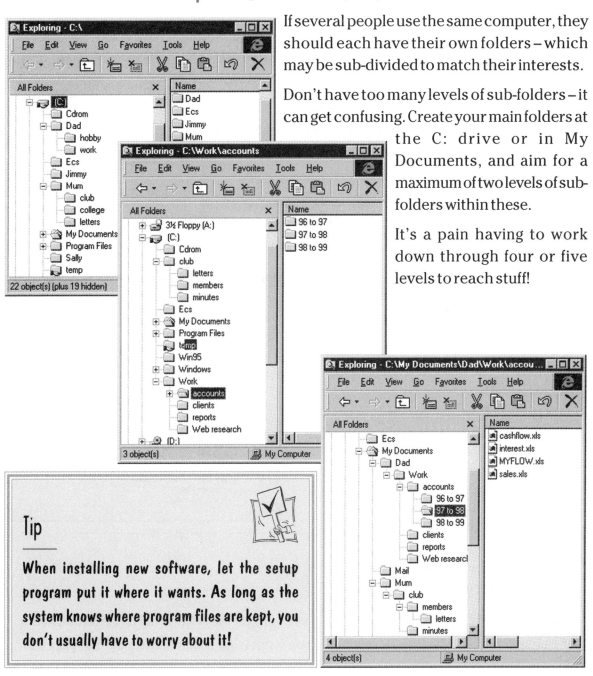

Tip

When installing new software, let the setup program put it where it wants. As long as the system knows where program files are kept, you don't usually have to worry about it!

Moving folders

Those of us who are less organised set up our new folders when the old ones get so full that it is difficult to find things. Nor do we always create them in the most suitable place in the tree. Fortunately, Windows 98 caters for us too. Files can easily be moved from one folder to another (see *Moving and copying*, page 58), and folders can easily be moved to new places on the tree.

In this example, *graphics* is being moved from within My Documents to become a top level folder on Drive C:.

(see *Moving and copying*, page 58)

Basic steps

1 Arrange the display so that you can see the folder you want to move and the place it has to move to.

2 Drag the folder to its new position, *making sure the target is highlighted.*

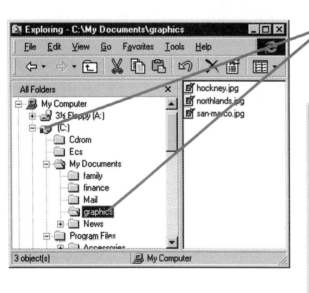

Can you see the folder and its target?

Drag to the target

Tip

Copying a folder – and all its files – to another disk can be a quick way to make a backup of a set of files.

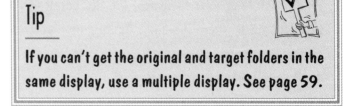

Tip

If you can't get the original and target folders in the same display, use a multiple display. See page 59.

See page 59.

Basic steps

1 Select the folder.

2 Check the files list. Are there any there? Do you want any of them? No, carry on.

3 Right-click on the folder to open the context menu or open the **File** menu and select **Delete**.

4 If necessary, you can stop the process by clicking **No** when you are asked to confirm that the folder is to be thrown in the Bin.

This is not something you will do every day, for deleting a folder also deletes its files, and files are usually precious things. But we all acquire programs we don't need, keep files long past their use-by dates, and sometimes create unnecessary folders.

● Don't worry about accidental deletions – files and folders deleted from your hard disk can be restored thanks to the Recycle Bin. (See page 61.)

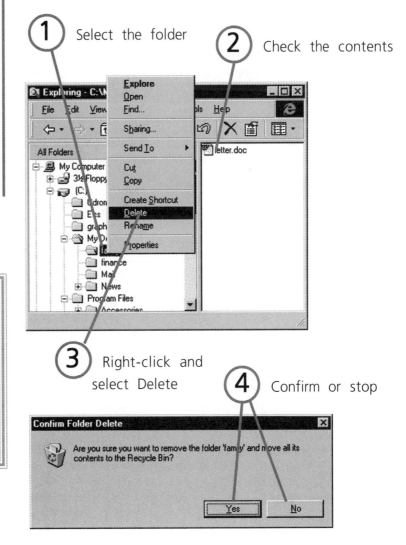

① Select the folder

② Check the contents

③ Right-click and select Delete

④ Confirm or stop

Tip

You can also delete folders – and files – by dragging them directly to the Recycle Bin (see page 61).

My Computer

At its default settings, the display of My Computer is simple, uncluttered and quite effective. You can see at a glance what files and folders are in the current folder – as long as there aren't too many! But sometimes, you need more control and more information.

The Toolbar has tools for all comon tasks, plus a (limited) means of changing folders. The folder list on the Toolbar only shows the drives and the folders in the path from the root to the current one.

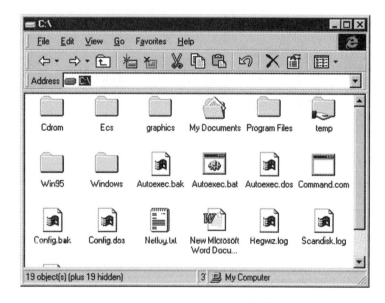

Use the drop-down list to switch to drives or folders higher up the same path

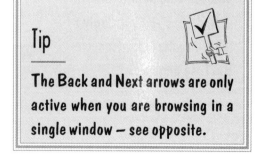

⇦ ▾	Go back to previous folder
⇨ ▾	Go to next folder
⬆	Go to parent folder
🖳	Map drives on a LAN (local area network)
🖳	Disconnect from LAN
✂	Cut – move folder or file to the Clipboard (see page 140)
📄	Copy file or folder
📋	Paste from Clipboard into current folder
↩	Undo last action
✖	Delete file or folder
📰	Display properties of file or folder
🗔 ▾	Alternative views of files (see page 41)

Tip

The Back and Next arrows are only active when you are browsing in a single window – see opposite.

Single window browsing

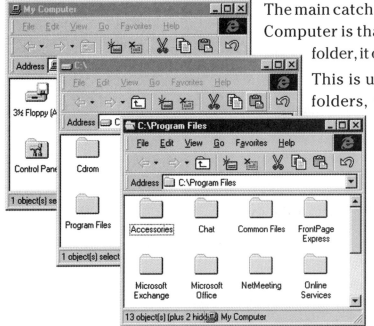

The main catch with the default settings in My Computer is that each time you go into a new folder, it opens another window.

This is useful if you want to open two folders, that both branch off from a previous one, so that you can move files from one to the other. It can be a nuisance, however, if you want to travel down the line to a third or fourth level folder. The screen clogs up with unwanted windows.

My Computer can be made to open each new folder in the same window.

There are two ways to do this:

- Hold down the **[Ctrl]** key when you click to open a new folder.

- The permanent fix – go to the **Folder Options**, select **Custom** and pick *Open each folder in the same window* on the **Custom Settings** panel (see page 42).

In single-window browsing the drop-down list on the Back button gives you quick access to the folders opened on the way down to the current one.

Once you have gone back, the Forward button and drop-down list also become active.

51

Summary

- ❑ You can use either **Explorer** or **My Computer** for managing your files and folders.

- ❑ The **Toolbar** gives you quick access to all the commonly-used commands.

- ❑ Disks are normally sub-divided into **folders**, to give organised storage for files.

- ❑ A folder's place in the system is identified by its **path**.

- ❑ A **filename** has two components, the name itself and an extension.

- ❑ The **name** can be as long as you like, and contain any mixture of letters, digits and symbols.

- ❑ **Extensions** are used to identify the nature of the file.

- ❑ You can control the display through the **View** and **Folder** options.

- ❑ Those files that are essential to the system are usually **hidden** from view. They can be brought into view, but should always be treated with respect.

- ❑ When you **create** a new folder, it will be placed on the branch below the selected folder.

- ❑ Try to keep your folder structure as simple as possible – you are going to have to find your way around your system!

- ❑ A folder, and its files, can be **deleted** or **moved** to a new position in the structure.

- ❑ **My Computer** can be set to run in a single or multiple windows.

5 Managing files

Arranging icons

Unless you specify otherwise, the Contents display lists your folders and files in alphabetical order–icons arranged across the screen; lists arranged in columns. Most of the time this works fine, but when you are moving or copying files, or hunting for them, other arrangements can be more convenient.

1 Open the **View** menu and point to **Arrange Icons**.

2 Select **by Name**, **Type**, **Size** or **Date**.

❏ **Details View**

3 Open the View menu and select **Details**.

4 To sort by **Name**, **Size**, **Type** or **Date**, click on the column header. Click twice to sort into reverse order.

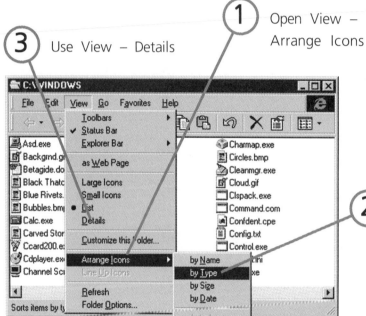

③ Use View – Details

① Open View – Arrange Icons

② Select the sort order

④ Click the header to sort on that column

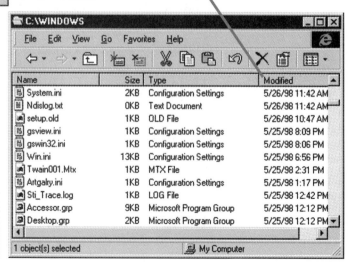

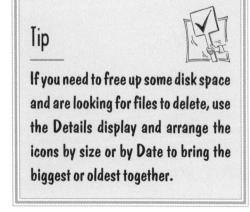

Tip

If you need to free up some disk space and are looking for files to delete, use the Details display and arrange the icons by size or by Date to bring the biggest or oldest together.

Basic steps

Improving visibility

❑ **Adjusting Details**

1 Point the cursor at the dividing line between two field headings.

2 When the cursor changes to ↔, drag the dividing line to change the width of the field on its left.

❑ **Adjusting the split**

3 Point anywhere on the bar between the panes to get the ↔ cursor.

4 Drag the shadowed line to adjust the relative size of the panes.

The amount of information in a My Computer or Explorer display can vary greatly, depending upon the number of items in a folder and the display style. You should be able to adjust the display so that you can see things properly.

As well as being able to adjust the overall size of the window, you can also adjust the width of each field in a Details display, and the split between the All Folders and Contents panes of Explorer.

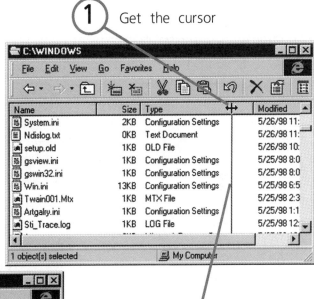

① Get the cursor

② Drag the line

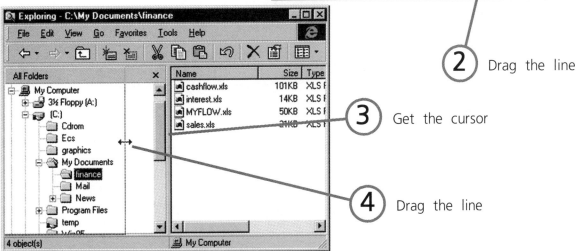

③ Get the cursor

④ Drag the line

Selecting sets of files

You can easily select single files by clicking on them, but you can also select groups of files. This is useful when you want to backup a day's work by copying the new files to a floppy disk, or move a group from one folder to another, or delete a load of files that are not wanted.

You can select:

- a block of adjacent files;
- a scattered set;
- the whole folder-full.

The same techniques work in Explorer and My Computer, with all display styles.

Basic steps

❏ **To select a block using the mouse**

1 Point to one corner of the block and click.

2 Hold down the mouse button and drag an outline around the ones you want.

❏ **[Shift] selecting**

3 Click on the file at one end of the block.

4 If necessary, scroll the window to bring the other end into view.

5 Hold **[Shift]** and click on the far end file.

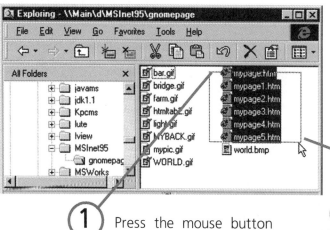

① Press the mouse button   ③ Click   ④ Hold [Shift]

Tip

Small icons and List views are best for these jobs!

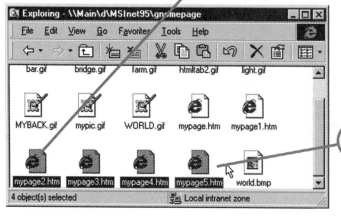

⑤ Click

Basic steps

❏ **To select scattered files**

1 Click on any one of the files you want.

2 Hold **[Ctrl]** and click each of the other files.

❏ You can deselect any file by clicking on it a second time.

❏ **To select all the files**

3 Open the **Edit** menu.

4 Choose **Select All**.

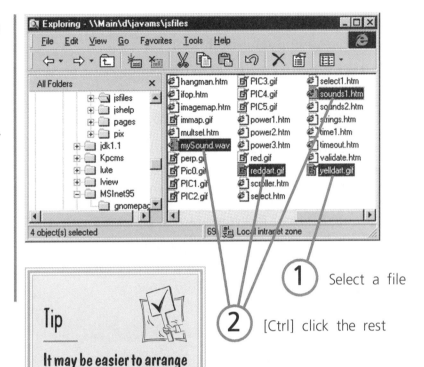

① Select a file

② [Ctrl] click the rest

Tip

It may be easier to arrange icons by **Name, Date** or **Type,** and **[Shift]** select.

③ Open the Edit menu

④ Choose Select All

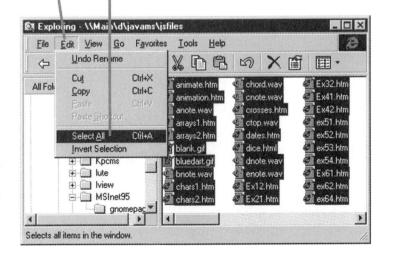

Tip

If you want all the files except for a scattered few, select those few, then use **Edit – Invert Selection** to deselect them and select the others.

Moving and copying

When you drag a file from one place to another, it will either move or copy the file. In general:

- It is a **move** if you drag to somewhere *on the same disk.*

- It is a **copy** if you drag the file *to a different disk.*

When you are dragging files within a disk, you are usually moving to reorganise your storage; and copying is most commonly used to create a safe backup on a separate disk.

If you want to move a file from one disk to another, or copy within a disk, hold down the right mouse button while you drag. A menu will appear when you reach the target folder. You can select Move or Copy from there.

1 Select the file(s).

2 Scroll the **All Folders** list so that you can see the target folder – don't click on it!

3 Point to one of the selected files and drag to the target.

or

4 Hold down the right mouse button while you drag then select **Move** or **Copy**.

❏ **Copying to a floppy**

5 Right click on the file to open its context menu, point to **Send To** and select the destination drive.

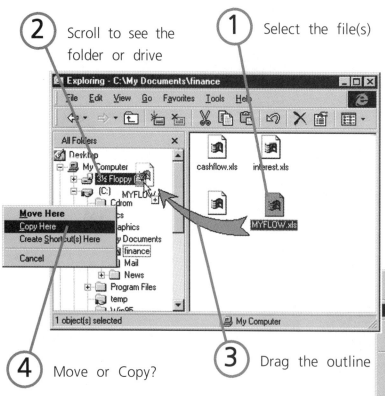

② Scroll to see the folder or drive

① Select the file(s)

④ Move or Copy?

③ Drag the outline

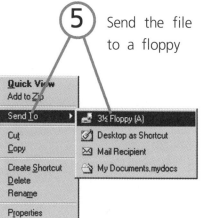

⑤ Send the file to a floppy

Multiple windows

1 Open Explorer or My Computer windows for the source and destination folders.

2 Select the file(s).

3 Drag the files to their destination.

If you want to copy to a folder on a floppy, or you are having difficulty arranging the Explorer display so that you can see the source files and the target folder, the simplest approach is to use multiple windows. Use either Explorer or My Computer.

① Open two windows

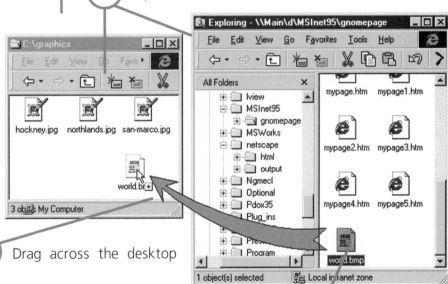

③ Drag across the desktop

② Select the files

Basic steps

Using the Clipboard

1 Select the file(s).

2 *Move* with **Edit – Cut**.
or
Copy with **Edit – Copy**.

3 Go to the destination.

4 Give the **Edit – Paste** command.

Windows 98 allows you to move and copy files and folders, as well as text, graphics and other data, through an area of memory called the Clipboard (see page 140).

The Cut, Copy and Paste commands are on the Edit menu of all Windows applications. Use them to copy within a disk, or move files to another disk – or for all your copying and moving, if you don't like dragging.

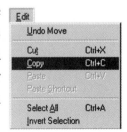

Deleting files

Thanks to the Recycle Bin, deleting files is no longer the dangerous occupation that it used to be – up to a point! Anything that you delete from the hard disk goes first into the Bin, from which it can easily be recovered. Floppies are different. If you delete a file from a floppy it really does get wiped out!

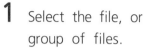

1 Select the file, or group of files.

2 Drag them to the **Recycle Bin** on the Desktop or in Explorer.

or

3 Press [**Delete**].

4 At the **Confirm** prompt, click **Yes** or **No** to confirm or stop the deletion.

① Select the files

③ Press [Delete]

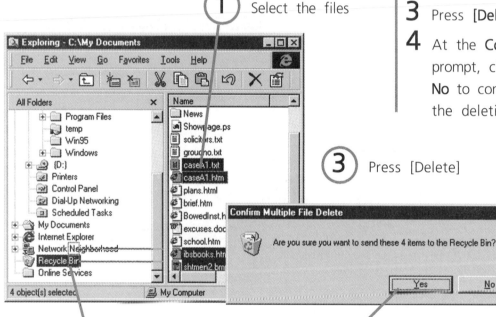

② Drag to the Bin

④ Confirm

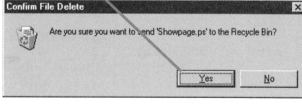

With single deletions, the filename is displayed; with multiple deletions you just get the number of selected files.

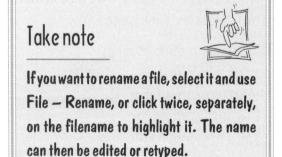

Take note

If you want to rename a file, select it and use File – Rename, or click twice, separately, on the filename to highlight it. The name can then be edited or retyped.

Basic steps

1 Open the Recycle Bin from the icon on the desktop or from Windows Explorer.

2 Select the files that were deleted by mistake – the **Original Location** field shows you where they were.

3 Right-click for the Context menu or open the **File** menu and select **Restore**.

This is a wonderful feature, especially for those of us given to making instant decisions that we later regret. Until you empty the Bin, any 'deleted' files and folders can be instantly restored – and if the folder that they were stored in has also been deleted, that is re-created first, so things go back into their proper place.

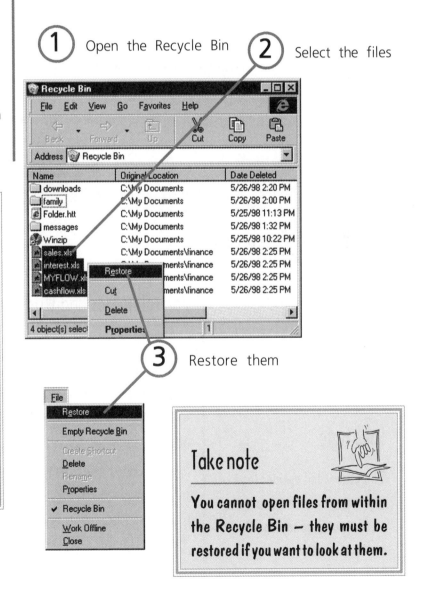

① Open the Recycle Bin ② Select the files

③ Restore them

Tip

Files sent to the Recycle Bin stay there until you empty it. Do this regularly, to free up disk space. Check that there is nothing that you want (Restore any files if necessary) then use File – Empty Recycle Bin.

Take note

You cannot open files from within the Recycle Bin – they must be restored if you want to look at them.

Finding files

If you are well organised, have a clear and logical structure of folders and consistently store your files in their proper places, then you should rarely need this facility when hunting outside your system. However, if you belong to the other 90% of users, you will be grateful for this.

- Find can track down files by name, type, age, size or contents. As long as you have something to go on, no files need remain lost for long.

- You can run Find from Explorer or the Start menu.

Basic steps

☐ **Finding by name**

1 From **Explorer**, open the **Tools** menu and select **Find**.

or

2 Click on **Start** and select **Find**.

3 Pick **Files or Folders...**

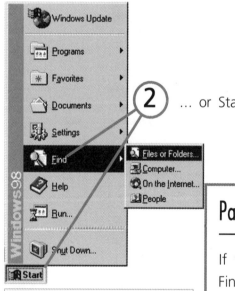

1 Use either Tools – Find ...

... or Start – Find

3 Select Files or Folders

Partial names and Wildcards

If you just type part of a name into the Named slot, Find will track down any file with those characters anywhere in the name.

e.g. '**DOC**' will find 'My **Doc**uments', 'Letter to **doc**tor', and all Word files with a .**DOC** extension.

If you know the start of the name and the extension, fill the gap with the wildcard *****. (include the dot!)

e.g. *REP*.TXT* will find 'REPORT MAY 15.*TXT*', 'REPLY TO IRS.**TXT**' and similar files.

Take note

The other Find options lead to panels, to find a computer on a network, or people or files on the Internet.

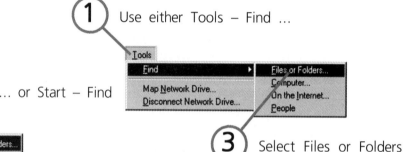

4 Type as much of the name as you know into the **Named** slot.

5 Select the drive from the **Look in** list or click **Browse** if you want to restrict the search to a particular folder.

6 Click [Find Now].

7 Double click the file to run it or open it with its associated program.

or

8 Click to select it and pull down the **File** menu. This has most of the Explorer filing options on it, and also allows you to open the file's folder.

④ Type part or all of the name

⑤ Select the drive or folder

⑥ Start the search

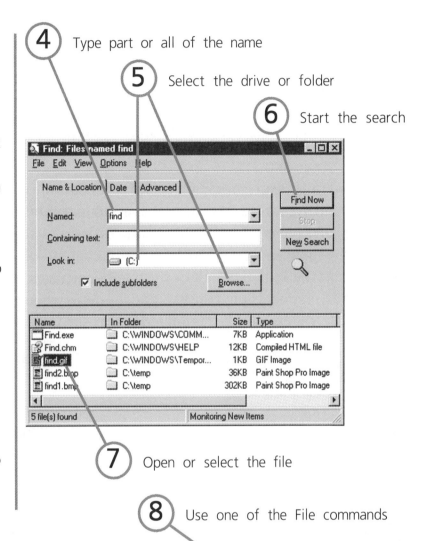

⑦ Open or select the file

⑧ Use one of the File commands

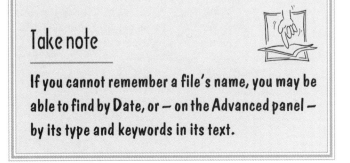

Take note

If you cannot remember a file's name, you may be able to find by **Date**, or – on the **Advanced panel** – by its type and keywords in its text.

Properties

As we saw on page 8, everything in Windows 98 has Properties. If you open the Properties box for any file, you will see a General panel, containing information about the file and some controls. Some files have additional panels.

● Program files have Version panels carrying product details;

● Word-processor, spreadsheet and other data files created by newer applications have Summary and Statistics panels. Summary information is created by the application's user to describe the contents of the file; the Statistics include the number of pages, words, characters and the like, and the dates when the file was created, last modified or accessed.

● Shortcuts have their own special panels (see next pages).

Basic steps

1 Select the file and click the 📋 Tool.

or

2 Right-click the file and select **Properties** from the short menu.

3 If you want to prevent the file from being edited, tick the **Read Only** checkbox.

4 Click tabs to open other panels, if present.

5 Click [OK] or [×] to close.

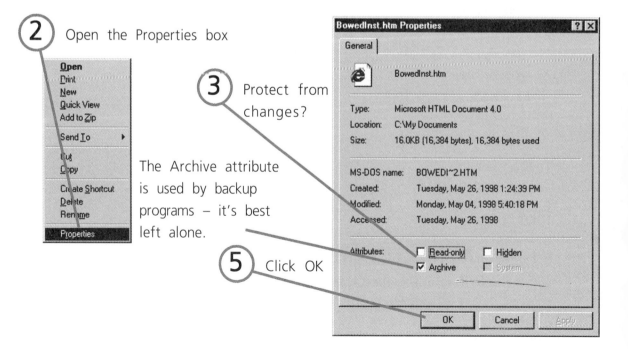

② Open the Properties box

③ Protect from changes?

The Archive attribute is used by backup programs – it's best left alone.

⑤ Click OK

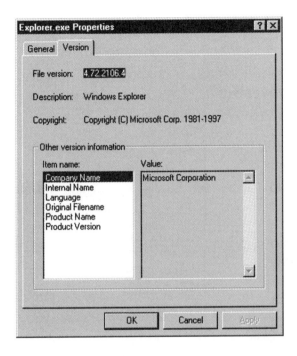

The **Version** panel (left) can tell you more about when and by whom a program was created. As its name implies, it is particularly useful for checking which version of a program you have.

The **Summary** panel (below) displays information written into it while the file was open in its application. This can be edited – click Apply or OK to save the revised information.

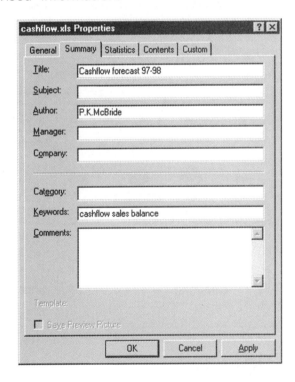

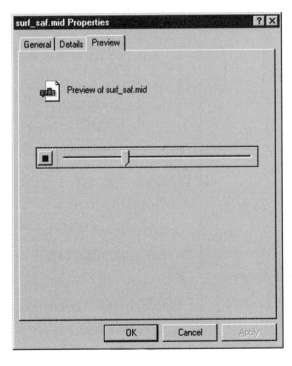

Some files will have Preview panels where you can see – or listen to – the contents.

Shortcuts

You can run a program by double-clicking on its EXE file in Explorer or My Computer, but Shortcuts make it easier. Shortcuts can be added to the Start menu (see page 92) or placed directly on the Desktop. This is a very convenient way of running programs that you use regularly.

You can set up a shortcut in a minute – and if you don't make much use of it, you can remove it even faster!

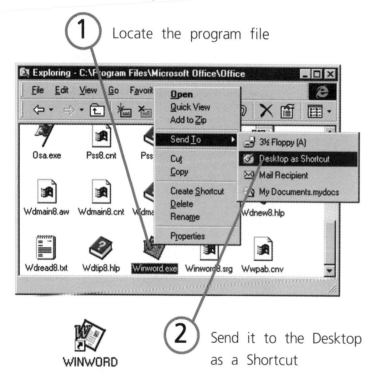

① Locate the program file

② Send it to the Desktop as a Shortcut

WINWORD

Take note

Too many shortcuts will clutter up your Desktop. Remove excess ones by selecting them and pressing [Delete]. This does not remove the program – only the shortcut.

1 Use **Explorer** or **My Computer** to find the program file – it will have an EXE or COM extension.

2 Right-click on the file to open its context menu and select **Send To** then **Desktop as Shortcut**.

or

3 Put the window into Restore mode so you can see some Desktop.

4 Drag the program icon onto the Desktop. This creates a Shortcut – it does not move the file.

5 Shortcuts created this way have a name starting with 'Shortcut to...' – edit the name.

6 Open the icon's **Properties** box and click the **Shortcut** tab.

❑ **Editing Properties**

7 Change the **Start in** folder, **Run** mode or **Icon** as required.

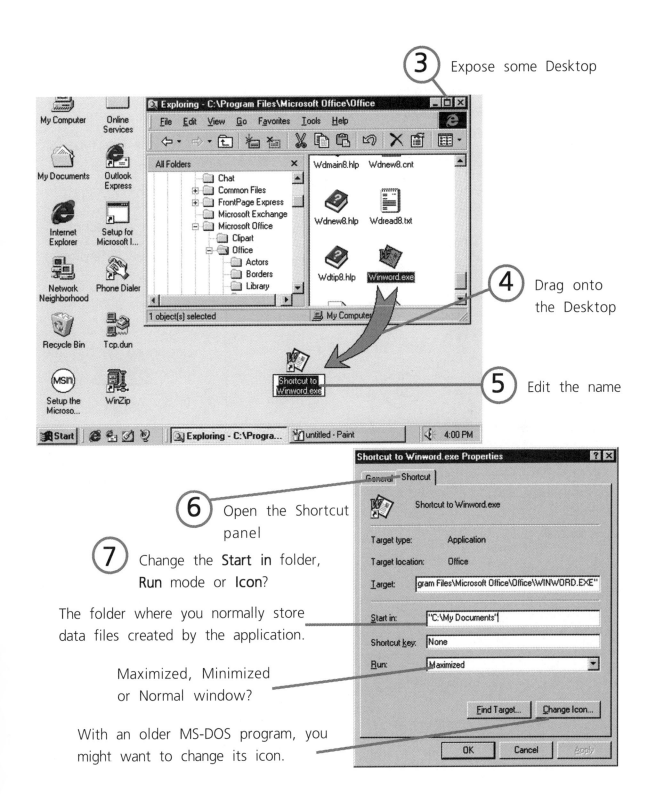

3 Expose some Desktop

4 Drag onto the Desktop

5 Edit the name

6 Open the Shortcut panel

7 Change the **Start in** folder, **Run** mode or **Icon**?

The folder where you normally store data files created by the application.

Maximized, Minimized or Normal window?

With an older MS-DOS program, you might want to change its icon.

67

File Types

Windows 98 keeps a list of registered file types. These are ones that it knows how to describe and how to handle. If you open a document of a known type, the system will run the appropriate application and load in the file. Windows 98 comes with a good long list, and you can teach it about new types through one of the Folder Options panels.

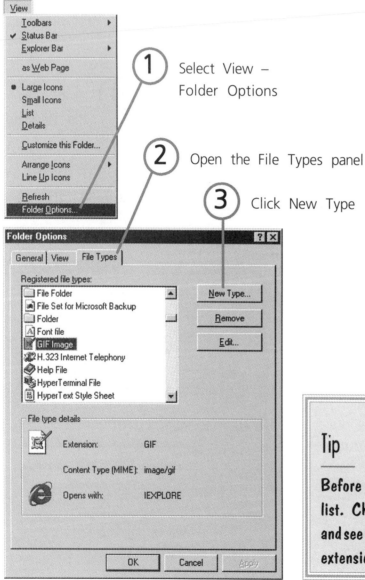

Select View – Folder Options

Open the File Types panel

Click New Type

Basic steps

1 Open the **View** menu and select **Folder Options...**

2 Click the **File Types** tab to open its panel.

3 Click New Type....

4 Type in a **Description**.

5 Enter the **Extension**(s) that mark this type.

6 You must define the Actions that can be performed on this file. Click New....

7 In the **Action** slot, type '*open*'.

8 Go to the application slot then Browse... through your folders and select it.

9 Click OK.

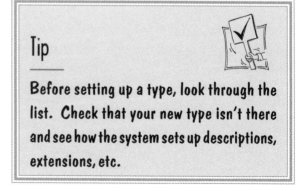

Tip

Before setting up a type, look through the list. Check that your new type isn't there and see how the system sets up descriptions, extensions, etc.

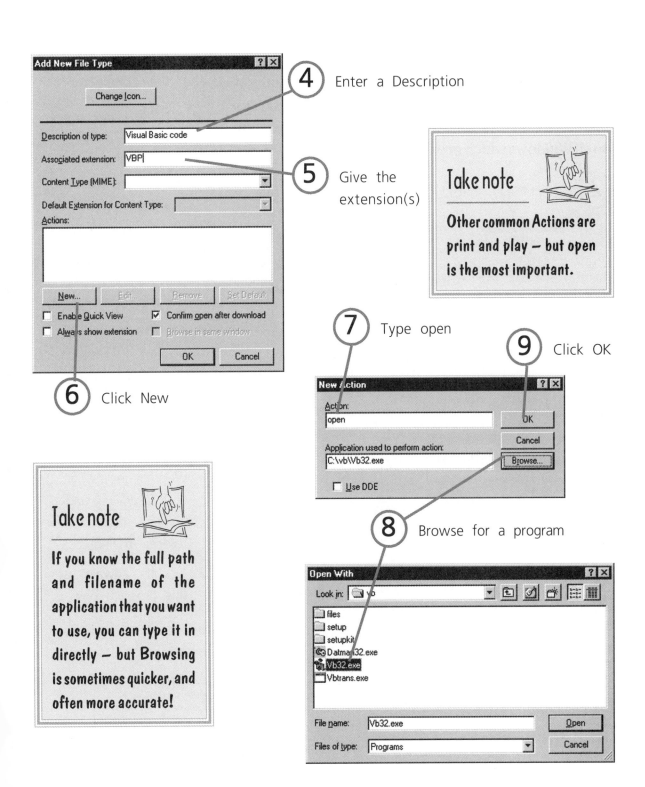

④ Enter a Description

⑤ Give the extension(s)

Take note

Other common Actions are print and play – but open is the most important.

⑥ Click New

⑦ Type open

⑨ Click OK

⑧ Browse for a program

Take note

If you know the full path and filename of the application that you want to use, you can type it in directly – but Browsing is sometimes quicker, and often more accurate!

Open With...

The Folder Options File Type panel offers a thorough, if slightly long-winded, means of registering new types. A simpler alternative is to wait until you come across unknown types of file, and then use the Open With routine to tell Windows which programs to use.

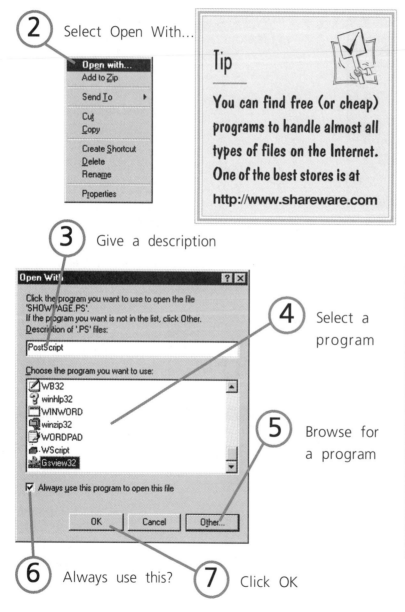

(2) Select Open With...

Tip

You can find free (or cheap) programs to handle almost all types of files on the Internet. One of the best stores is at

http://www.shareware.com

(3) Give a description

(4) Select a program

(5) Browse for a program

(6) Always use this?

(7) Click OK

Basic steps

❏ Opening With ...

1 Right click on a file to get its context menu. If the first item is **Open**, Windows knows how to handle it – stop now!

2 Select **Open With..**

3 At the **Open With** dialog box, type a **Description**. This will be used in Details displays in Explorer.

4 Scroll through the list and pick the program to use with this file.

5 If you can't find the program in the list click ▢ Other... ▢ and browse through your folders to find it.

6 Tick the **Always use this program** box, if relevant – sometimes you may want to use the same file with different programs.

7 Click ▢ OK ▢

70

Basic steps

Editing a type

1 Select the type.

2 Click [Edit...].

Either

3 Change the **Content Type** or **Extension**.

or

4 Select an action and click [Edit...] to link a new program.

Whether you set up your new type through the View Options, or through Open With, it is possible that it may need some fine tuning later. Errors must be corrected, and established file types may also need editing over time as you replace programs with newer versions, but still retain the data files.

The Edit panel is reached through Folder Options – File Types.

(1) Select the type

(2) Click Edit

Folder Options `[?][X]`

General | View | **File Types**

Registered file types:

- MSN Central
- MSN Phone Book
- My Documents
- Outlook Express Mail Message
- Outlook Express News Message
- **Paint Shop Pro Image**
- PCX Image Document
- PostScript
- PSP Browser File

[New Type...] [Remove] [Edit...]

File type details

Extension: EPS BMP WPG PNG WMF

Content Type (MIME): image/jpeg

Opens with: PSP

[OK] [Cancel] [Apply]

Tip

Sometimes it is quicker to remove a type definition and start from scratch, rather than to edit it.

(4) Change the Content or Extension

Edit File Type `[?][X]`

[Change Icon...]

Description of type: Paint Shop Pro Image

Content Type (MIME): image/jpeg

Default Extension for Content Type: .jpeg

Actions:

- **open**
- print
- printto

.jpe
.jpeg
.jpg
.LBM

[New...] [Edit...] [Remove] [Set Default]

☐ Enable Quick View   ☑ Confirm open after download
☐ Always show extension   ☐ Browse in same window

[OK] [Cancel]

(3) Edit an action

71

Summary

❑ You can **arrange icons** by Name, Type, Size or Date.

❑ Files and folders can be displayed as **icons** or in **lists with details**.

❑ You can use [Shift] to **select a block of files**, or [Ctrl] to **select a scattered set**. A block of files can also be selected with the mouse.

❑ **Dragging a file** will normally move it within the disk, or copy it to a floppy.

❑ By holding the **right button** as you drag, you can copy within a disk or move to a floppy.

❑ To **delete** a file or folder, press [Delete]. If the file was on the hard disk, it is sent to the **Recycle Bin**, from which it can be recovered. Files deleted from a floppy really are deleted.

❑ The **Find** utility will help you to track down files if you have forgotten where you put them, or what they were called.

❑ The **Properties** box of a file can be a useful source of information.

❑ You can create **Shortcuts** to programs and place them on your desktop for quick and easy access.

❑ If Windows 98 knows about a **file type**, it knows how to describe it and what program to open it with. You can teach the system about new types.

❑ When you try to open a file of an unknown type, you will get the **Open With...** option and can then tell it which program to use.

6 Exploring the Internet

Online services

Before you can do anything on the Internet, you must have a connection to it through an Internet Access Provider. If you do not have one already, the Online Services folder has all you neeed to connect to any one of half a dozen services. Try CompuServe or AOL – both offer a month's free trial to prospective members.

Basic steps

1 Put your Windows CD-ROM in the drive.

2 Go to the **Programs – Online Services** menu and select a service.

3 Wait while the setup runs, responding to any prompts.

4 Use the **Sign Up** entry to join the service.

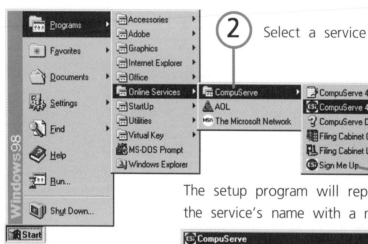

(2) Select a service

The setup program will replace the service's name with a menu

(4) Sign Up

Tip

To learn about the Internet, read *The Internet Made Simple.*

74

Basic steps

1 Run Internet Explorer and go online.

2 From **Start** select **Windows Update** – from the main menu or from **Settings**.

3 Wait while the **Update Wizard** scans your system.

4 If you want an update select it and click **Install** then wait for it to download and install itslef.

One of the first things that you should do, once you have your connection to the Internet, is go to Microsoft's Windows Update site to see if there are any new or improved routines for Windows 98.

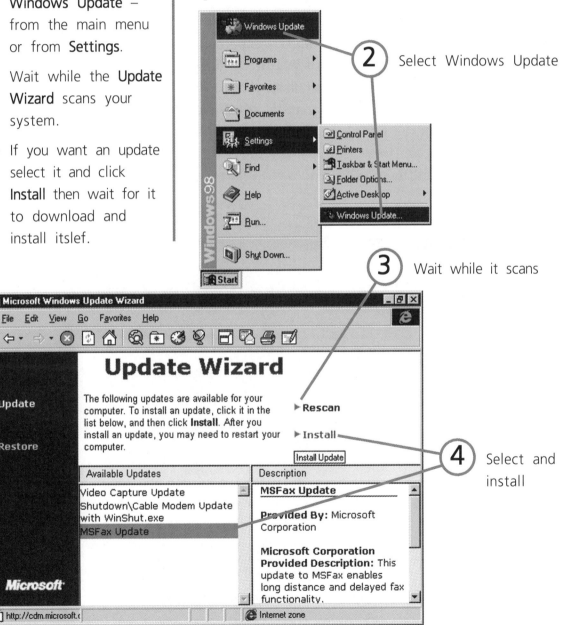

② Select Windows Update

③ Wait while it scans

④ Select and install

Internet Explorer

If you want to view pages on the World Wide Web, you need a browser. Internet Explorer is the one integrated into Windows 98. (In fact, if you open a Link, Favorite or Channel from Windows Explorer and My Computer, the Internet Explorer toolbar will replace the normal one.)

Internet Explorer was designed to be – and is – easy to use. The Explorer Bar offers a simple way to **Search** the Net, to visit **Favorite** places, retrace your steps (**History**) or access the **Channels**. Pick up a link from the Bar and it is displayed in the main screen. There are ready-made links to start you off on your browsing, and there's plenty of help available online at Microsoft – and many other places on the Internet.

Basic steps

1 Run Internet Explorer from the **Desktop**, the **Quick Launch Taskbar Toolbar** or the **Programs** menu.

2 Click on a **Link**.

or

3 Search for material.

or

4 Type in an **Address**.

(4) Type in an Address (3) Start a search (2) Click on a Link

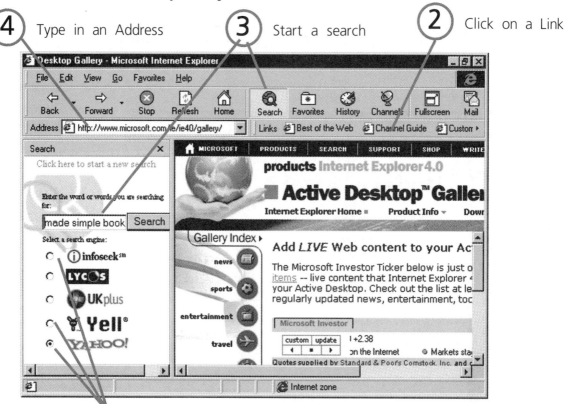

Yahoo is the Net's greatest organised directory; use UKplus for general UK stuff; Yell for UK businesses; Infoseek and Lycos cover virtually the whole Web between them

The Full Screen tool removes everything except the main toolbar to give maximum viewing area.

The Explorer Bar can be closed down for a better view of Web pages. This is one of the 'Best of the Web' pages at Microsoft – a good place to start browsing.

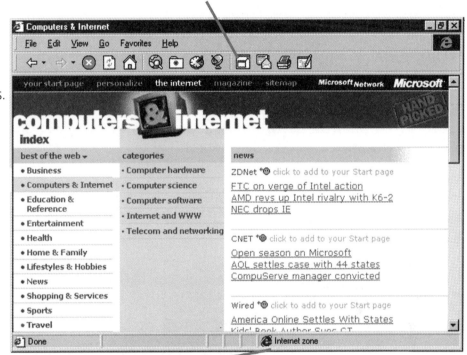

Internet Explorer is strong on security. You can set it so that it will only access only named sites in the *Trusted* zones. You can also set it up to prevent children from reaching sites with unsuitable content.

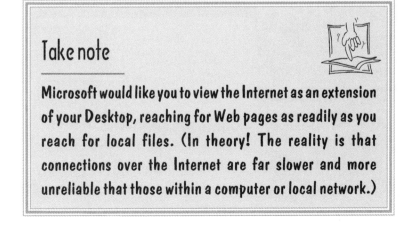

Take note

Microsoft would like you to view the Internet as an extension of your Desktop, reaching for Web pages as readily as you reach for local files. (In theory! The reality is that connections over the Internet are far slower and more unreliable that those within a computer or local network.)

Tip

If you want to know more, try *Internet Explorer Made Simple* by Sam Kennington.

Favorites

With millions of Web pages available, finding really good ones can take time. When you do find them, you should add them to the Favorites list so that you can get back to them quickly in future. Internet Explorer has a few Favorites set up for you, to start you off.

You can access Favorites directly off the Start menu – you must be online before you select one – but the best way to use them is to open the Favorites list in the Explorer Bar in Internet Explorer.

Basic steps

1 Click **Start**, point to **Favorites**, then a folder and select one.

or

2 Run Internet Explorer.

3 Click on **Favorites**.

4 Open a folder.

5 Select a page.

You can customise the Start page to include only those features that you want, then make it your Home page, so your browsing always starts here.

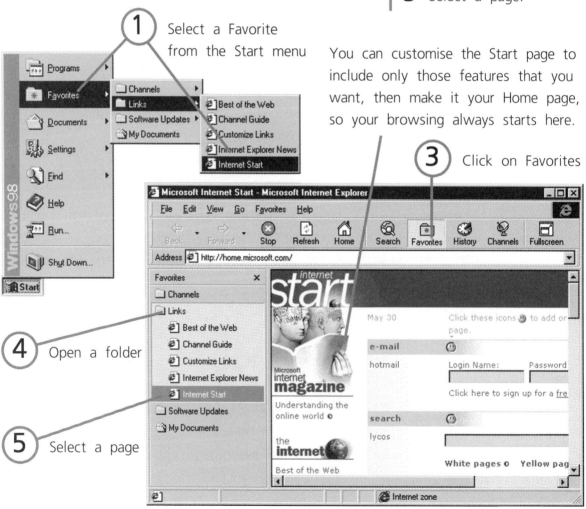

Select a Favorite from the Start menu

Open a folder

Select a page

Click on Favorites

Outlook Express

The World Wide Web may be the most important aspect of the Internet, but it is not the only one. The other two major aspects are e-mail and the newsgroups (where enthusiasts exchange ideas on specific topics).

Outlook Express will handle your e-mail and newsgroup access efficiently. Messages can be composed and read offline, so that you only need to connect briefly once or twice a day to send and receive new ones – keeping phone bills to a minimum.

The Subject lines of messages are shown here. They tell you who sent the article, when, and what it's about. Select one to read it in the lower pane.

Folders for your mail and selected newsgroups are listed here.

This pane also acts as a word-processor when you are writing your own messages.

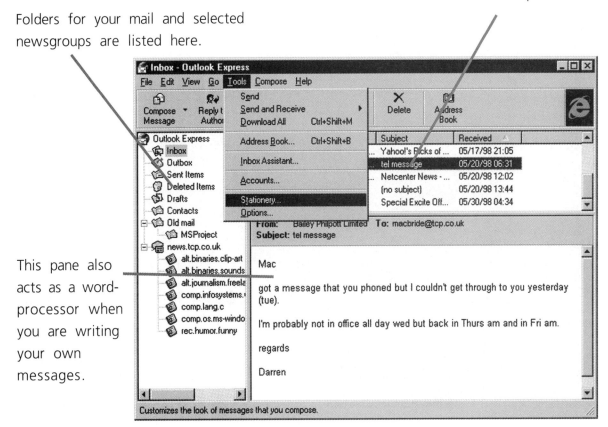

Channels

The theory behind channels is this: instead of you having to go to sites to see what's happening, you get them to send you regular updates of new material, which you can then read offline. It works well if you are in an organisation with a permanently open connection, as the updates can be scheduled to come in while you are doing other things.

If you connect through a dial-up line, the channel approach is not so good. It is more efficient to go to a site to collect the material you want than to have a channel pour in stuff that may or may not be of interest.

Basic steps

❑ **Adding a channel**

1 Put your Windows 98 CD-ROM in the drive.

2 Click on the Channel Bar to open it in Explorer.

3 Open a folder.

4 Select a channel and wait for its lead page to load from the CD.

5 Click Add Channel and choose how to handle its update.

② Open the Channel Bar in Explorer

③ Open a Folder

④ Select a channel

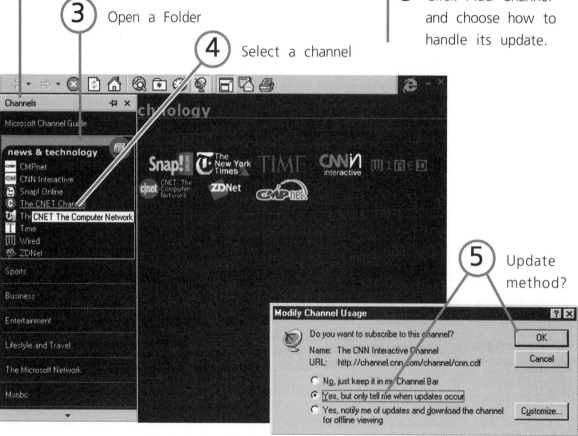

⑤ Update method?

Basic steps

❏ **Updating a channel**

1 Go online.

2 Open a **Favorites** menu and select **Manage Subscriptions**.

3 Right-click on the channel and select **Update Now**.

3 Wait – the first download may be very slow!

4 Browse the channel, going online if you want to follow up links.

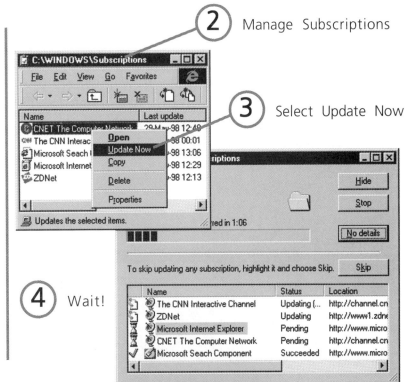

② Manage Subscriptions

③ Select Update Now

④ Wait!

⑤ Browse the new pages

Channels usually download the top pages and headlines – to follow the stories you need to go online

Active Desktop

The Active Desktop can hold interactive links to sites. There are a range of items available at Microsoft's Active Desktop Gallery – including the Search Component shown here. This gives you a simple way to hunt through dozens of the different search engines – sites that have indexes to Web pages, newsgroups and other Net resources.

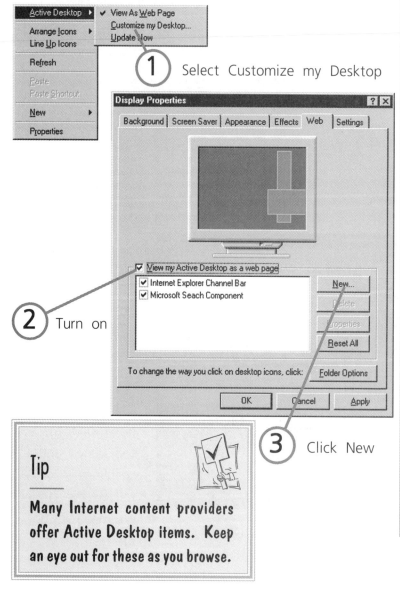

Select Customize my Desktop

Turn on

Click New

Tip

Many Internet content providers offer Active Desktop items. Keep an eye out for these as you browse.

❑ **Adding a channel**

1 Right-click on the Desktop, point to **Active Desktop** and select **Customize...**

2 Turn on **View ... as a Web page**.

3 Click New... and wait for the Gallery to download.

4 Select an item and click Add to Active Desktop and wait for it to download.

❑ **Using the Search component**

5 Go online.

6 Select a Search Engine.

7 Type in one or more words to define what you are looking for.

8 Click Go ▶. Internet Explorer will open, linking to Microsoft, then on to the search engine, to find and display the results.

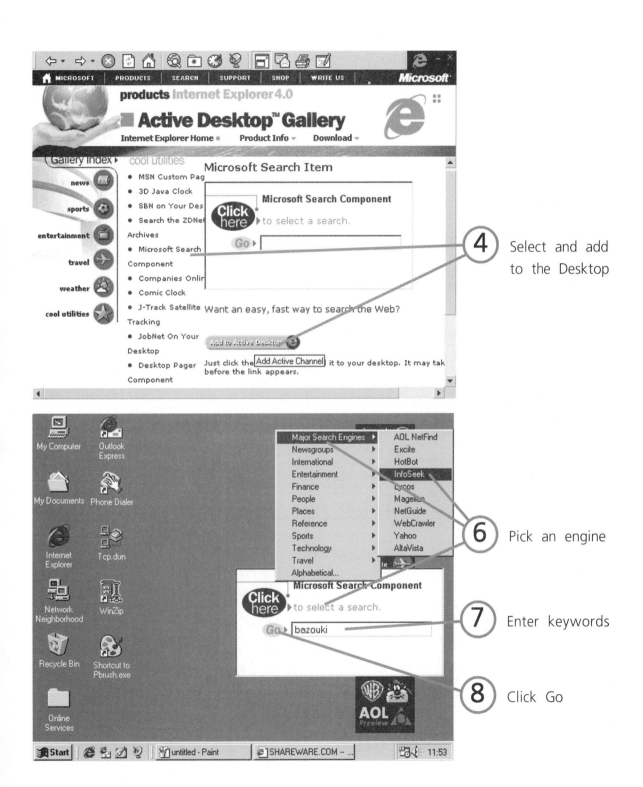

Select and add to the Desktop

Pick an engine

Enter keywords

Click Go

83

Netscape

Internet Explorer is not the only browser! Netscape Navigator is an excellent alternative, and one preferred by many people. It is also the one favoured by more Web page authors, so there are more sites geared to use its special features than those of Internet Explorer.

Netscape Navigator is currently supplied as part of a comprehensive Internet suite, Communicator, which also includes mail and news software, an HTML page editor and Netcaster (for channel), plus 'net phone', real-time conferencing and Web chat utilities. If you just want a browser and mail/news software, the earlier Netscape 3.0 is equally good.

It's easy to install – and to uninstall if you decide that you do not like it.

Tip

If you find that you prefer it to Internet Explorer, take a few moments to work through the File Types (in the Folder Options) and edit those that open with Internet Explorer so that they use Netscape instead.

The layout and tools are very similar to those of Internet Explorer – Bookmarks are the equivalent of Favorites

Easy access to the other Communicator programs

Clear, attractive toolbar icons and well organised menu systems are a feature of all the Netscape programs.

A screenshot from **Messenger**, the mail and news software in the Communicator suite. As you can see, you can use it to read – and write – messages with formatted text and embedded images. Like Outlook Express, Messenger allows you to read and write message offline.

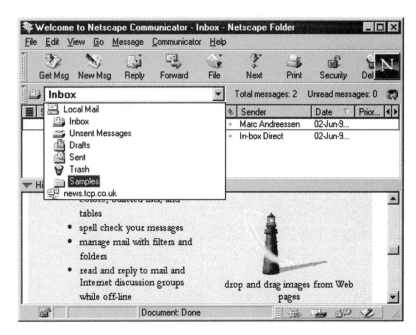

Take note

If you would like to try Netscape Navigator, you can often find it on the CDs on computer magazines. You can also download it from Netscape's home site at:

http://www.netscape.com

or wherever you see the button. The full Communicator package is over 10Mb, but the earlier – and excellent – Navigator 3.0 is around 5Mb.

Tip

If you want to know more about the Netscape browsers, try *Netscape Made Simple* or *Communicator Made Simple* by Sam Kennington.

Summary

❑ If you do not yet have an Internet Access Provider, try one of those in the **Online Services** folder.

❑ Go online to the **Windows Update** site from time to time to see if Microsoft has any new or improved versions of its Windows 98 software.

❑ **Internet Explorer** is the supplied Web browser. It is fully integrated with My Computer and Windows Explorer, so you can also start to browse from there.

❑ The **Favorites** folder stores links to selected places on the Internet. There are some already set up and you can add your own links.

❑ **Outlook Express** is the supplied software for handling e-mail and newsgroup articles.

❑ If you subscribe to **Channels**, you can have the latest material from sites sent directly to your Desktop.

❑ Items added to your **Active Desktop** will give you interactive links to sites.

❑ Netscape is well worth investigating as an alternative to Internet Explorer.

7 The Taskbar

Taskbar options

Many parts of the Windows 98 system can be tailored to your own tastes. Some of the most important are covered in the next two chapters. We'll start with the Taskbar and the Start menu. You can adjust the size of the menu icons, turn the clock on or off, hide the Taskbar, or place it on any edge of the screen.

❏ **Adjusting the display**

1 Click ![Start].

2 Point to **Settings**.

3 Click on **Taskbar & Start Menu...**

4 Set an option.

5 Click [Apply] to see how it looks.

6 Click [OK] to fix the settings and close.

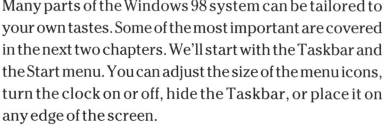

Point to Settings

Click on Taskbar

Start here

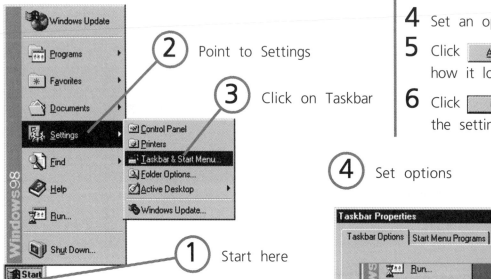

④ Set options

Always on Top – when off, to see the Taskbar you must minimise applications or press [Ctrl]-[Esc]

Auto hide slides the Taskbar off-screen when not in use. Point to off-screen to restore the Taskbar to view.

Small icons in Start menu gives a far more compact main menu

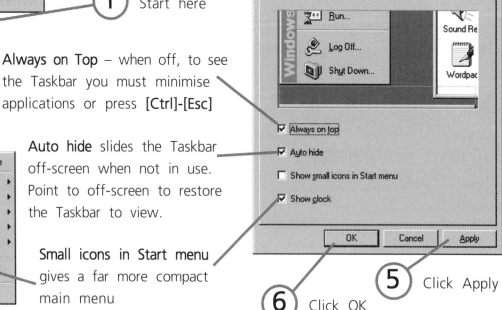

⑤ Click Apply

⑥ Click OK

Basic steps

Moving

❏ **Moving**

1 Point to any free space on the Taskbar.

2 Drag towards the top, left or right of the screen, as desired.

3 Release the mouse button.

❏ **Resizing**

4 Point to the inside edge of the Taskbar.

5 When the cursor changes to ←→, drag to change the width of the Taskbar.

Moving and resizing

Moving the Taskbar is quite easy to do by mistake, so it is just as well to know how to do it intentionally – if only to correct a mistake!

Resizing the Taskbar – making it deeper, or wider – is sometimes useful. Narrow vertical displays are almost unreadable.

When you are running a lot of programs with a horizontal Taskbar, the titles on the buttons can be very small. If you deepen the display, you get two rows of decent-sized buttons.

Take note

If you like to keep the Taskbar visible, it takes least space at the top or bottom of the screen.

If you have a lot of applications running at once, or several toolbars on the Taskbar (see page 90), then the Taskbar is best at the left or right edge, but with Auto-Hide turned on.

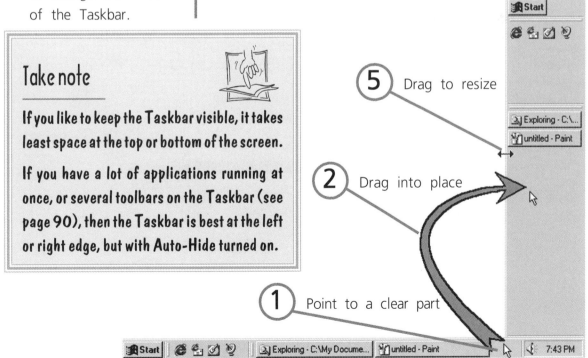

⑤ Drag to resize

② Drag into place

① Point to a clear part

Taskbar Toolbars

The normal setting for the Taskbar is to have the Quick Launch Toolbar, plus buttons for any open applications and the Clock.

If you find that you do not use it, Quick Launch can be removed, to allow more space for application buttons.

If you like working from the Taskbar, other Toolbars can be added, turning the Taskbar into the main starting point for all your commonly-used activities.

□ **Adding Toolbars**

1 Right-click on an empty place on the Taskbar to open its context menu.

2 Point to **Toolbars.**

3 Click on a Toolbar to add it to (or remove it from) the Taskbar.

□ **Toolbar options**

4 Right-click on a Taskbar Toolbar to open its context menu.

5 Point to **View** and set the button size.

6 Turn on the Toolbar **Title** if required.

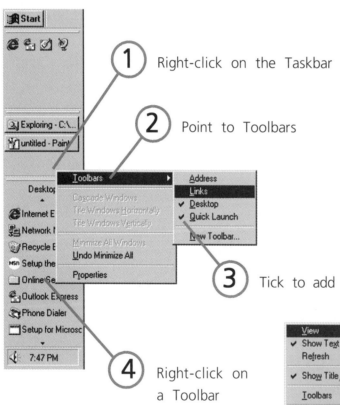

① Right-click on the Taskbar

② Point to Toolbars

③ Tick to add

④ Right-click on a Toolbar

⑤ Set the button size

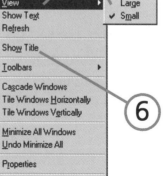

⑥ Show the titles?

90

Basic steps

1 Create a new folder – it can be in any convenient place.

2 Set up shortcuts to you main programs.

3 Open the Taskbar menu, point to **Toolbars** and select **New Toolbar**.

4 Select your new folder.

5 Click [OK].

Tip

If you add toolbars to the Taskbar, a horizontal display will get too crowded to see things properly. Drag it to a side position, make it wide enough for the buttons to fit and turn on Auto-Hide.

Creating a new toolbar

If you like the Taskbar as a means of starting programs, you can set up new Taskbar Toolbars to hold your own collections of shortcuts to programs that you use regularly.

① Create a folder

② Set up shortcuts

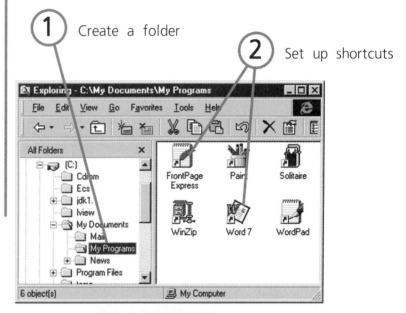

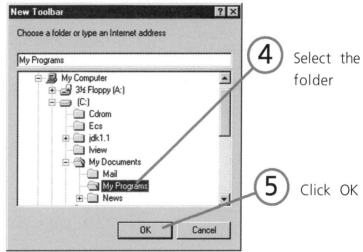

④ Select the folder

⑤ Click OK

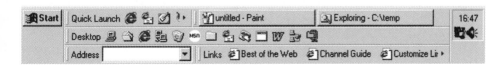

The Start menu

When Windows 98 was installed onto your system, it created a Start menu that included shortcuts to all its own applications and accessories. If you had upgraded from Windows 95, it will have included all the entries in the old Start menu. If you had been running Windows 3.1, it will have taken your Program Manager groups and incorporated them into the Start menu structure. When you install new software onto your system, the installation routine should also bring them into the Start menu.

If it gets built automatically, why would we want to mess around with it? The answer is that installation routines can only do so much. They may not structure the menus as you would like. Not all software comes with a routine to install it into Windows 98.

The Start Menu Programs panel of the Taskbar Properties box gives you control of your menu structure.

Use these buttons to change the entries on your menus

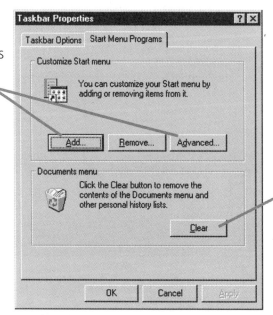

Click here if you ever want to remove all the Documents entries from the Start menu — there's not usually much point, as newer ones will constantly replace the older entries.

Basic steps

1 Click [Add...].

2 Click [Browse...] and work through your folders to find and select the program.

3 Select the menu folder to hold the new entry.

4 Replace the program's filename with a more meaningful name.

You can add individually, any programs that were not handled by the installation routines. All that is essential is that you know where to find them.

You can type the path and filename if you know it

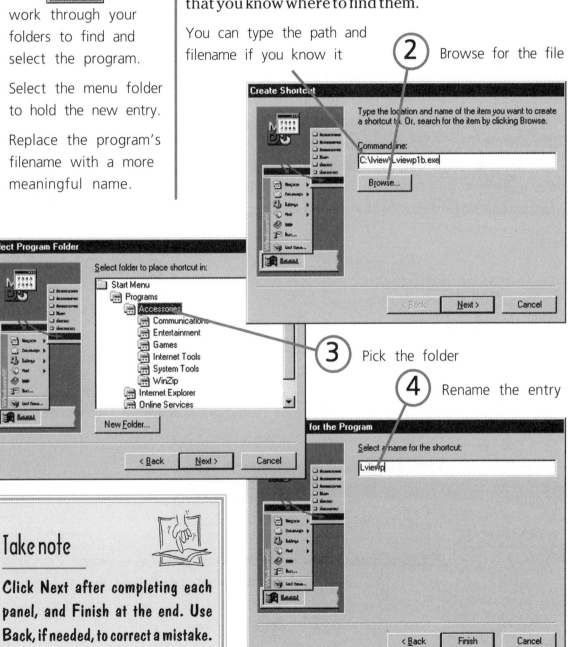

2 Browse for the file

Create Shortcut

Type the location and name of the item you want to create a shortcut to. Or, search for the item by clicking Browse.

Command line:

C:\lview\Lviewp1b.exe

Browse...

< Back   Next >   Cancel

Select Program Folder

Select folder to place shortcut in:

- Start Menu
  - Programs
    - Accessories
      - Communications
      - Entertainment
      - Games
      - Internet Tools
      - System Tools
      - WinZip
    - Internet Explorer
    - Online Services

New Folder...

< Back   Next >   Cancel

3 Pick the folder

4 Rename the entry

for the Program

Select a name for the shortcut:

Lviewp

< Back   Finish   Cancel

Take note

Click Next after completing each panel, and Finish at the end. Use Back, if needed, to correct a mistake.

Organising the menu

The Advanced button takes you into Explorer, with the focus on the Start menu folder. From here you can rename, reorganise, delete, create new shortcuts and move them into menu folders. The one job you are most likely to want to do is reorganise.

When you run the installing routine for new software, it will typically create one or more menu entries or a new folder in the Programs menu. This is all well and good, but after a while the Programs menu can get huge – I've seen them wrap twice around the screen! Setting up new sub-menus, and grouping related items onto them will give you a far neater and more usable menu system.

Basic steps

☐ **Making a sub-menu**

1 Click [Advanced...].

2 Select the **Programs** folder.

3 Open the **File** menu and select **New – Folder**.

4 Rename the folder.

5 Select the relevant folders and entries and drag them onto the new folder.

6 Close **Explorer**.

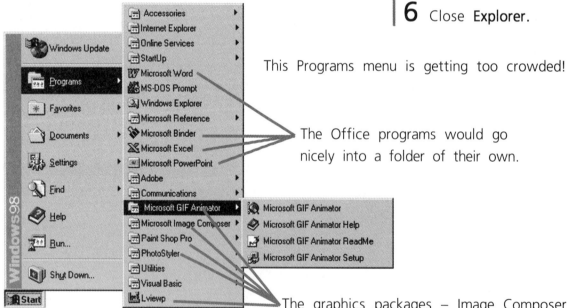

This Programs menu is getting too crowded!

The Office programs would go nicely into a folder of their own.

The graphics packages – Image Composer, GIF Animator, Paint Shop Pro, PhotoStyler and Lview – could be grouped together onto a Graphics menu.

94

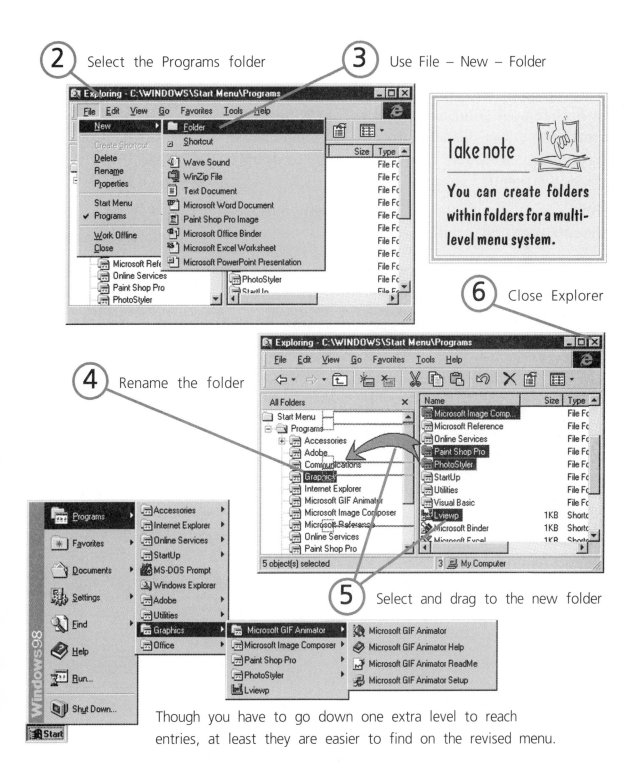

② Select the Programs folder

③ Use File – New – Folder

Take note

You can create folders within folders for a multi-level menu system.

⑥ Close Explorer

④ Rename the folder

⑤ Select and drag to the new folder

Though you have to go down one extra level to reach entries, at least they are easier to find on the revised menu.

95

Removing entries

If you remove software from your system, you may also need to remove its entry from the Start menu – uninstall programs don't always do a clean sweep. You may also want to remove some of the entries that Windows 98 created when it was installed. If necessary, programs can be added back onto the menu later, or run by double-clicking on them in Explorer.

Don't worry too much about deleting entries by mistake – the entries go first to the Recycle Bin.

Basic steps

1 Click [Remove...].

2 Open up sub-folders if necessary, until you can see the entry.

3 Select the entry.

4 Click [Remove...].

5 Repeat Steps 2 to 4 remove all unwanted entries.

6 Click [Close] to return to the Properties panel.

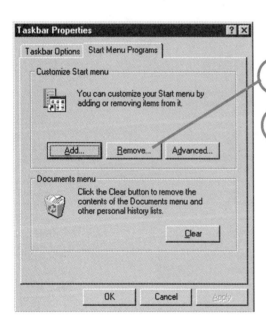

① Click Remove

② Open folders as necessary

③ Select the entry

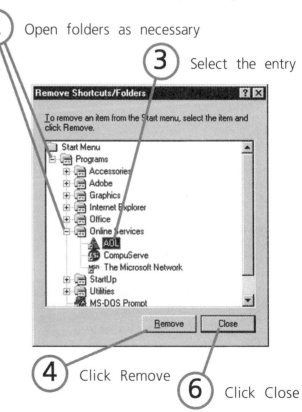

④ Click Remove

⑥ Click Close

Take note

You can remove whole folders – and their entries – if you need to.

Basic steps

1 Right-click on the clock to open its context menu.

2 Select **Adjust Date/ Time**.

3 Pick the **Month** from the drop-down list.

4 Click on the **Day**.

5 Click on **Hour**, **Minute** or **Second** to select then either adjust with the arrows or type the correct value.

6 Click [Apply] to restart the clock.

Setting the Clock

We can't leave the Taskbar without having a look at adjusting the Date and Time. This should not need doing often – PCs keep good time, and Windows 98 even puts the clock forward and back for Summer Time!

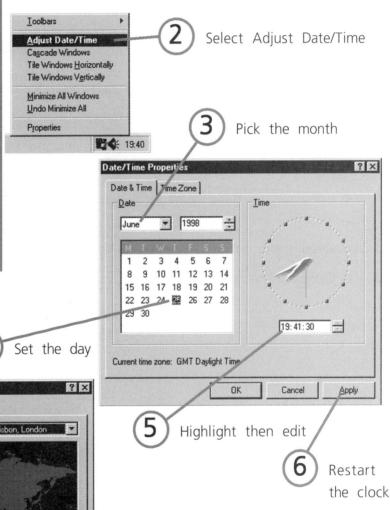

② Select Adjust Date/Time

③ Pick the month

④ Set the day

⑤ Highlight then edit

⑥ Restart the clock

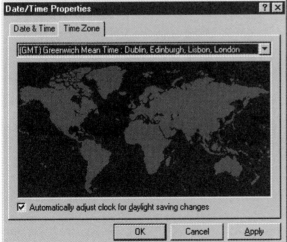

If you want to change the **Time Zone**, pick the zone from the drop-down list.

Summary

❑ The **Taskbar** can be reduced to a thin line or allowed to lie behind active windows, but is easiest to use if it is visible and always on top.

❑ The Taskbar can be **moved** to any edge of the screen, and **resized** if needed.

❑ The **Start menu** is a folder in the Windows folder. Its entries are folders or shortcuts to programs. It can be managed through Explorer or My Computer, but changes are simpler through the Settings.

❑ You can **add new entries** to the menu by creating shortcuts and storing them in a chosen folder.

❑ The menu can be **reorganised** by moving entries to new or other existing folders.

❑ **Unwanted menu entries** are easily removed.

❑ The **Clock** can be set by opening its short menu.

8 The Control Panel

The settings

The **Control Panel** allows you to customise many of the features of Windows to your own need and tastes.

Some settings are best left at the defaults defined by Windows 98; some should be set when new hardware or software is added to the system; some should be set once then left alone; a few can be fiddled with whenever you feel like a change.

Nine of those control settings that can or should be adjusted are covered in this section.

Date/Time see *Setting the Clock* page 97

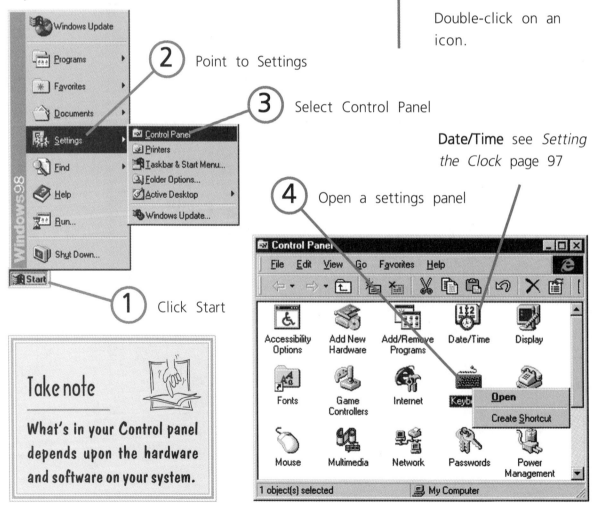

Basic steps

1 Click **Start**.

2 Point to **Settings**.

3 Select **Control Panel**.

Either

4 Right-click an icon and **Open** it from the short menu.

or

Double-click on an icon.

> **Take note**
>
> **What's in your Control panel depends upon the hardware and software on your system.**

Display

The Display

This may seem to be pure frills and fancies, but it does have a serious purpose. If you spend a lot of time in front of your screen, being able to see it clearly and use it comfortably is important.

Background panel

The **Wallpaper** is the background to the desktop. Some are hideous, but others are acceptable. The supplied designs can be edited with Paint, if you feel artistic, or you can use any bitmapped graphic of your own. With a large image, set it in the **Centre** rather than duplicate it as a **Tile**.

If you prefer a single colour background, you may want to impose a **Pattern** on it.

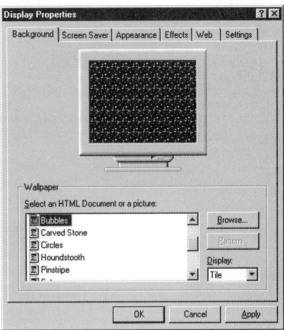

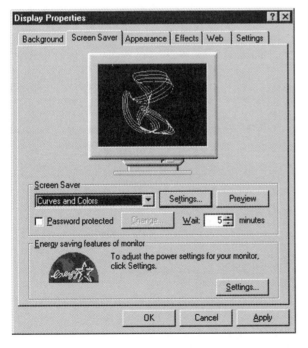

Screen Savers

These are fun but serve little real purpose nowadays. (On an old monitor, if a static image was left on too long, it could burn into the screen.) A screen saver switches to a moving image after the system has been left inactive for a few minutes. **Preview** the ones that are on offer. **Settings** allows you to adjust the images.

There is a small industry churning out weird and wonderful screen savers for you to buy, if you want something different.

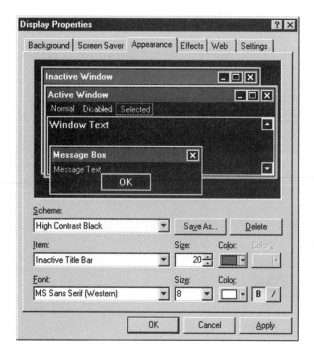

Appearance

This controls the colour schemes and the size of fonts. There is a set of ready-made schemes, or you can select individual parts of the screen from the **Item** list and adjust the **Colour** or **Font**. The scheme can then be saved with a new name.

There are **High Contrast** and coloured **Large** and **Extra large** (font) schemes if easy viewing is needed.

If you make a mess of the scheme – easily done! – restore the appearance by selecting the **Windows Standard**.

Effects

Don't like the standard Desktop icons? Here's your chance to change them. You can pick from a large set of alternatives or use icons that you have created or found on the Internet. If you are treating the screen as a Web page, the icons may get in the way and can be turned off.

The Visual Effects are mainly cosmetic. Large icons are useful as part of a high visibility scheme. The remaining options produce a slicker, smoother display, though they make the system work a little harder.

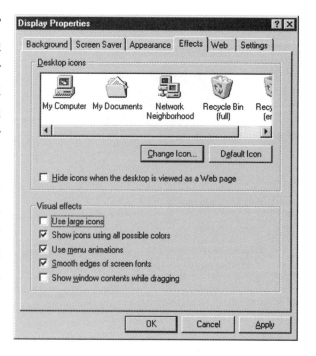

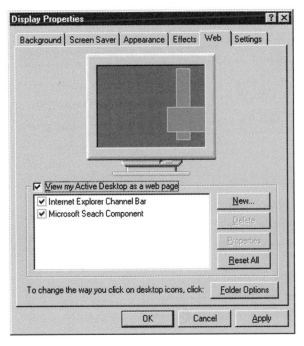

Web

This panel controls the key **Active Desktop** settings. If you do not want the active integration with the Internet, turn off the **View as a web page** option. Otherwise, start here to add new elements to your Desktop (see page 82).

The **Reset All** button will remove all active elements, apart from the Channel Bar, and restore the default background.

You can also reach this panel from the Start menu, through the Settings–Active Desktop–Customize my Desktop sequence.

Settings

Play with the other panels as much as you like, but treat this one with respect. In particular, leave the **Advanced** options alone unless you are unhappy with the current display *and* know what you are doing. You can switch to a display mode that it not properly supported by your hardware, resulting in a screen which is difficult or impossible to read – and therefore to correct!

If you do produce an unreadable screen, reboot the system using the Startup disk – you did make one, didn't you – and restore the default setting from there.

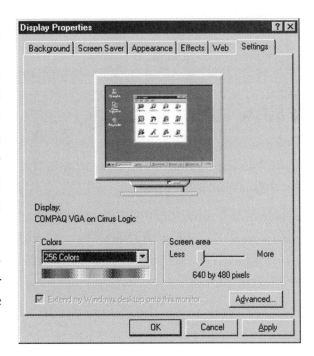

Adjusting the mouse

Mouse

Don't change to **Left-handed** unless you are the only one who uses the system, and it is the only system that you use. You will only confuse yourself and others.

The **Double-Click Speed** determines the difference between a proper double click and two separate clicks.

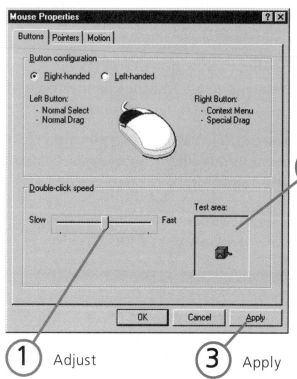

① Adjust

③ Apply

Pointer Speed links speed and distance, so that the faster you move the mouse, the further the pointer goes.

*Find Pointer and Double-click speeds that suit you and **stick with them**. If you keep fiddling with these, you will never get the feel of the mouse.*

Pointer Trails make the mouse easier to see on the LCD screens of portables.

- ❏ Buttons panel
1 Set the **Double-click** speed.
2 Double-click in the **Test** area to see if the system responds.
3 Click [Apply].
- ❏ Motion panel
4 Set the **Pointer Speed**.
5 Test it at the bottom of the panel.
6 Click [Apply].

④ Adjust   ⑤ Test

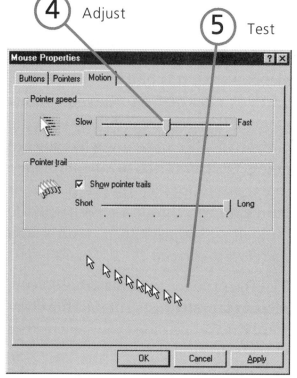

104

Basic steps

Pointers

□ **Pointers panel**

1 Pick a **Scheme**.

2 Select an action.

3 Click [B_rowse...].

4 Pick a cursor image for the action.

5 Click [_Open].

6 Repeat Steps 2 to 5 for any other actions.

7 Click [OK].

There are alternative Schemes, including ones with large and extra large pointers. You can also pick your own images (and animated ones with Microsoft Plus!) to link to chosen mouse actions.

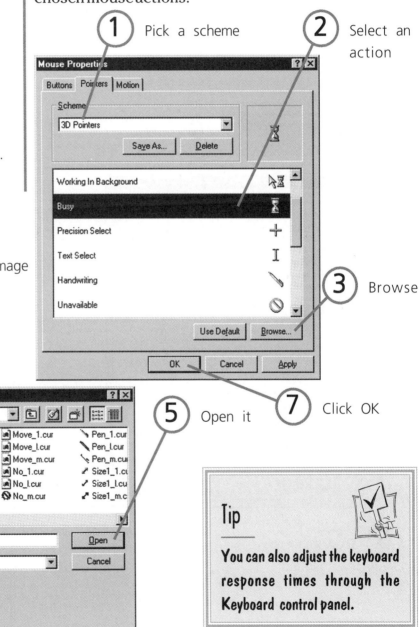

① Pick a scheme

② Select an action

③ Browse

④ Select an image

Check out the Preview

⑤ Open it

⑦ Click OK

105

Sounds

Windows allows you to attach sounds to events. These can be seen as useful ways of alerting you to what's happening or as more modern noise pollution. It all depends upon your point of view. I like a fanfare when the system is ready to start work (to wake me up – well, you wait so long!) and very few other sounds. But try them out – the Utopia sounds are worth listening to.

Basic steps

1 Pick a **Scheme**

2 Select an event.

3 Click ▶ to Preview its sound.

4 Sample a few more.

5 Go back to Step 1 and try alternative schemes until you have found the one you like best.

6 To set individual sounds, Browse for an alternative, or select [none] for the **Name**.

7 Click [Apply] or [OK].

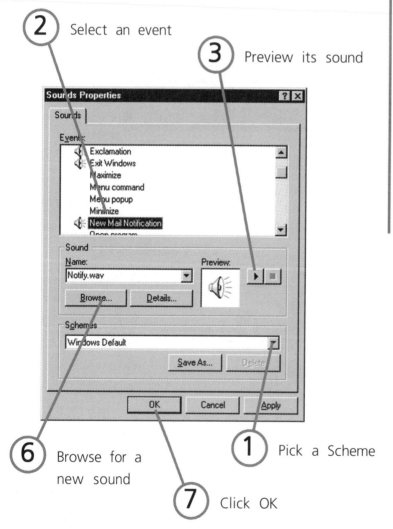

② Select an event

③ Preview its sound

⑥ Browse for a new sound

① Pick a Scheme

⑦ Click OK

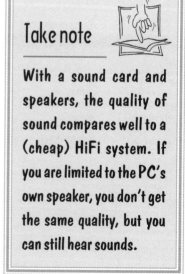

Take note

With a sound card and speakers, the quality of sound compares well to a (cheap) HiFi system. If you are limited to the PC's own speaker, you don't get the same quality, but you can still hear sounds.

Regional settings

Regional Settings

Basic steps

❑ Date styles

1 Run **Regional Settings**.

2 Open the **Date** panel.

3 Pick a **Short date style** from the list and edit it to your taste.

4 Click Apply.

5 Point to the Taskbar clock and see how it looks.

6 Repeat for the **Long date**.

These control the units of measurement and the styles used by most applications for displaying dates, time, currency and other numbers. The choice of Region in the top panel sets the defaults for the rest.

The other panels are for fine-tuning the styles. The **Date** panel is a good example. There are **Short date** and **Long date** styles. Both use the same coding:

Day	Month	
d	M	Number
dd	MM	Number with leading 0 if needed
ddd	MMM	Three letter name
dddd	MMMM	Full name

Year yy for 98; yyyy for 1998

2 Open the Date panel

3 Pick a style and edit

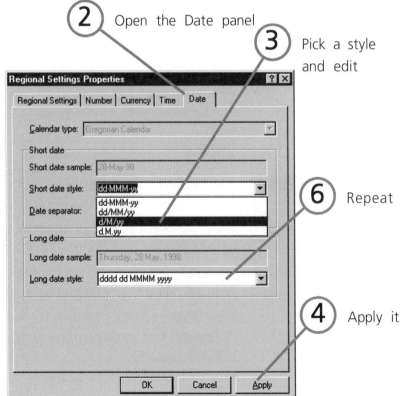

6 Repeat

4 Apply it

Take note

Setting the clock is covered on page 97.

5 Check it out

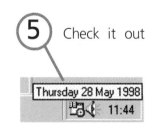

To get this, the Long date style was edited to:

dddd d MMMM yyyy

Accessibility

Accessibility
Options

These offer a range of ways to make life easier for people with sight, hearing or motor control disabilities – though the keyboard alternative to the mouse may well be useful to other people as well.

Keyboard

With **StickyKeys** you can type [Ctrl], [Shift] and [Alt] combinations by pressing one key at a time, rather than all at once.

FilterKeys solves the problem of repetition of keystrokes caused by slow typing.

ToggleKeys play sounds when any of the Lock keys are pressed.

Sound

These give visual alternatives to warning sounds and messages.

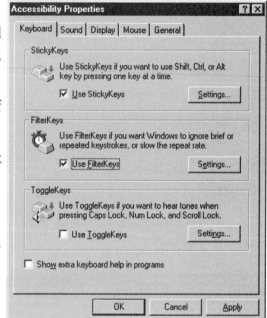

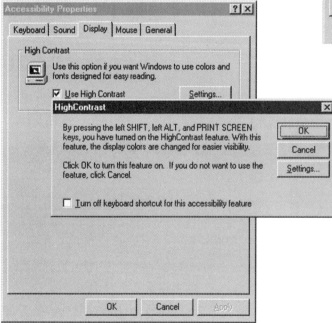

Display

The High Contrast displays can be selected from here, as well as from the Display panel. A special feature of this panel is that it allows you to set up a keyboard shortcut to toggle between High Contrast and normal displays – very useful if the computer has multiple users with different needs.

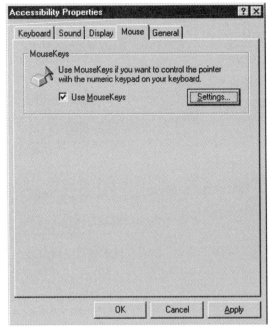

Mouse

With this feature turned on, the arrow keys on the Numeric keypad can be used to move the mouse, and the central [5] acts as the left mouse button. It is more limited than the mouse – you can only move up, down, left or right and not diagonally – but it is easier to control.

Click the **Settings** buttons and experiment to find the most workable levels.

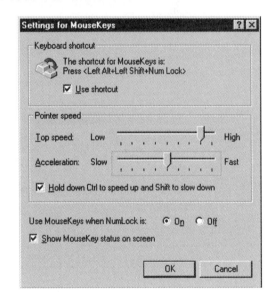

General

If you are using any of the Accessibility options, check this panel to make sure that they are turning on and off as and when you want them.

This illustration shows the standard High Contrast display setting. If required, larger fonts could be set for the panel and button text.

Add/Remove Programs

Any software written to the Windows 95/98 standards should be easy to install and – just as importantly – easy to remove. Unwanted parts of the Windows 98 can also be removed – and you can add accessories that were omitted during the initial installation.

❑ **Removing Programs**

1 Run **Add/Remove Programs**.

2 Select the program.

3 Click [Add/Remove..] and wait – you may be asked to confirm the removal of some files – if in doubt, keep them.

① Go to Add/Remove Programs

You can install from here, but it is simpler to use any new software's Setup routine

② Select the program

Some files may be left – check through Explorer

③ Click Add/Remove

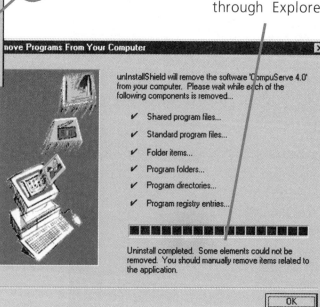

Take note

You may need the original disks or CD-ROM to uninstall some software.

❏ **Trimming Windows**

4 Go to **Windows Setup** and wait while it checks your system.

5 To remove an entire set of related files, click on the checkbox to clear it.

6 To remove individual files from a set, select the set and click 〔 Details... 〕.

7 Clear the checkboxes for unwanted items then click 〔 OK 〕.

8 At the main panel, click 〔 OK 〕 to start the removals.

Take note

To add new accessories or other features, tick the checkboxes instead of clearing them!

④ Go to Windows Setup

⑤ Clear to remove

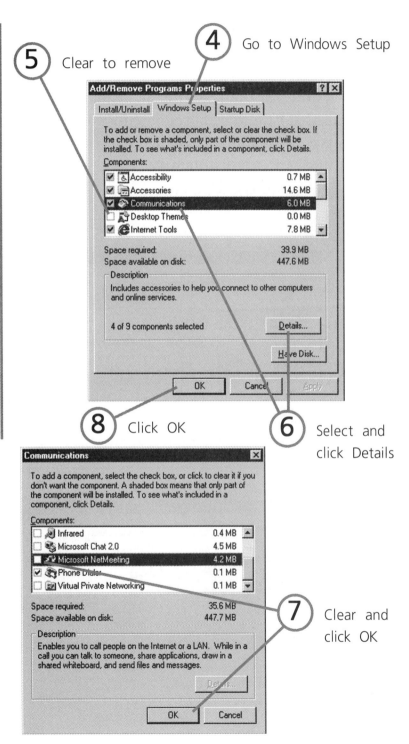

⑧ Click OK

⑥ Select and click Details

⑦ Clear and click OK

Fonts

Fonts

There is one school of thought that says you can never have enough fonts. There is a decent core supplied with Windows itself, and you will normally acquire more with any word-processor and desktop publishing packages that you install. If these are not enough for you, there are whole disks full of fonts available commercially and through the shareware distributors.

Installing new fonts is quick and easy.

❑ **Adding fonts**

1 Place the disk of new fonts into a drive.

2 Open the **File** menu and select **Install New Font**.

3 Select the drive and folder and wait while the system reads the names of the fonts on the disk.

4 Click ⟨ Select All ⟩, or work through the list and select the ones you want to install.

5 Click ⟨ OK ⟩.

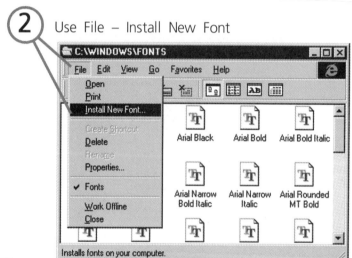

② Use File – Install New Font

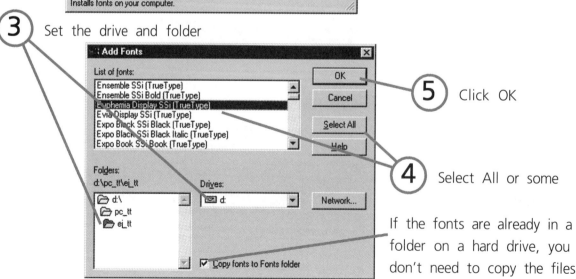

③ Set the drive and folder

⑤ Click OK

④ Select All or some

If the fonts are already in a folder on a hard drive, you don't need to copy the files

112

Basic steps

❑ **Font samples**

1 Click [AB] the **Similarity** tool.

2 Pick a font to **list by**, then select and **Open** it from its context menu.

3 Select and **Open** any *Very Similar* font.

4 Click [Done] to close the viewer.

5 If it is not useful, press [Delete] to remove it.

Removing unwanted fonts

This will save space on the hard disk, speed up Windows' Start Up and produce a shorter set to hunt through when you are setting a font in an application. Listing fonts by similarity helps to identify unnecessary ones.

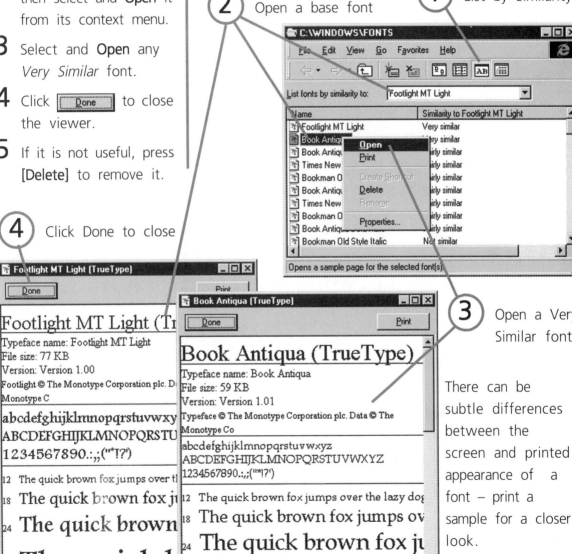

① List by Similarity

② Open a base font

④ Click Done to close

③ Open a Very Similar font

There can be subtle differences between the screen and printed appearance of a font – print a sample for a closer look.

Summary

❑ The **Control Panel** contains routines that determine the settings of some of the most basic features of how Windows works.

❑ The **Display** give you plenty of scope for personal preferences. Set the wallpaper, patterns, colour scheme and fonts to suit yourself – but don't change the Advanced Settings unless you have to.

❑ The key **Active Desktop** settings are controlled from the Display panel.

❑ Adjust the **mouse** and **keyboard** responses to your own needs at an early stage, then leave them alone.

❑ There are several **mouse pointer** schemes, and individual pointers can be redesigned.

❑ **Sounds** can be assigned to events, to alert you when things happen.

❑ The **Regional settings** control the appearance of dates, times, currency and numbers in most Windows Applications.

❑ Windows 98 has a number of **Accessibility Options** to make the screen easier to read and the mouse and keyboard easier to control.

❑ To delete unwanted software, or parts of the Windows 98 setup, use **Add/Remove Programs**.

❑ New **Fonts** can be installed easily. It is just as easy to examine fonts and to remove unnecessary ones.

9 Disk housekeeping

The System Tools

These programs will help to keep your disks in good condition, and your data safe.

Backup – provides a means of creating safe and compact backup copies of your files;

Disk Cleanup – finds and removes unused files;

Disk Defragmenter – optimises the organisation of storage to maximize the disk's speed and efficiency;

Drive Converter – (for systems upgraded from earlier versions of Windows) converts the file storage to the more efficient 32-bit format;

Scandisk – finds and fixes errors in data stored on disks;

Scheduled Tasks – lets you run the Tune-Up at set times;

System File Checker – checks essential files, restoring them if necessary;

System Information – gives (technical) information about what's going on inside your computer;

Windows Tune-Up – runs Disk Cleanup, ScanDisk and Disk Defragmenter. Can be set to run automatically.

Basic steps

1 Click **Start**..

2 Point to **Programs**

3 Point to **Accessories**.

4 Point to **System Tools**.

5 Click to select a tool.

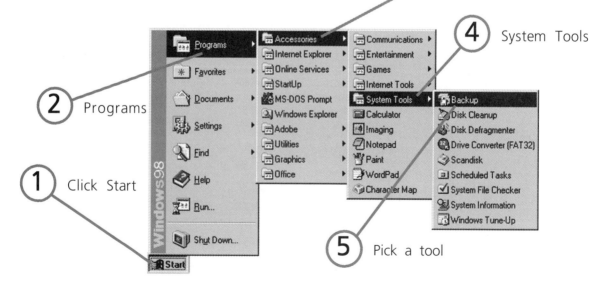

③ Accessories

④ System Tools

② Programs

① Click Start

⑤ Pick a tool

116

Basic steps

1 Open **My Computer**, right-click on the drive for the context menu.

2 Select **Properties**.

3 Bring the **Tools** tab to the front.

4 Select a tool.

Routine chores

The three system tools that are needed for the routine housekeeping chores can also be reached from the Properties box of any disk. The messages will remind you of chores you have been neglecting!

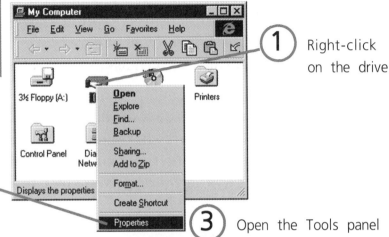

① Right-click on the drive

② Select Properties

③ Open the Tools panel

④ Pick a tool

This is Scandisk

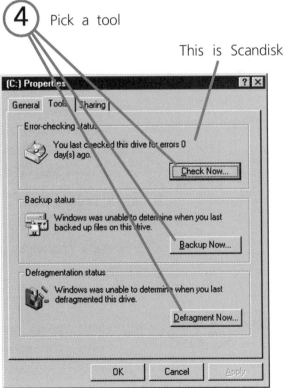

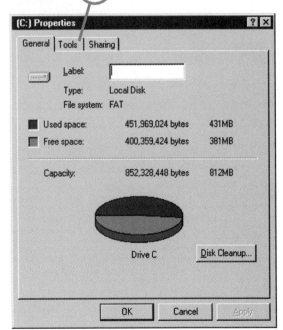

Use this panel to check how much space you have left on a disk.

Scandisk

Data is stored on disks in *allocation units*. A small file may fit on a single unit, but others are spread over many. A file's units may be in a continuous run or scattered over the disk (see *Disk Defragmenter*, page 124), but are kept together by links from one to the next. Sometimes these links get corrupted leaving *Lost fragments*, with no known links to any file, or *Cross-linked files*, where two are chained to the same unit of data. Scandisk can find – and often fix – these problems.

Sometimes the magnetic surface of the disk becomes corrupted, creating *Bad sectors* where data cannot be stored safely. Scandisk can identify these and, with a bit of luck, retrieve any data written there and transfer it to a safe part of the disk.

Basic steps

1 Run **Scandisk** from the Start menu or the disk's Properties box.

2 Select the **Drive** to be scanned.

3 Normally go for the quicker **Standard** scan, to fix file errors only. Do a **Thorough** scan to check for bad sectors on new disks and then every couple of months.

4 Set **Advanced** options as required – see opposite.

5 Click [Start].

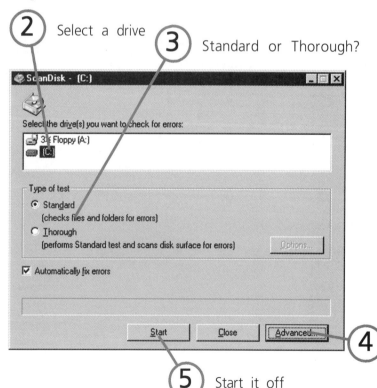

② Select a drive

③ Standard or Thorough?

④ Open the Advanced box

⑤ Start it off

Take note

If the Standard scan finds bad sectors, it will offer to run a Thorough scan to fix them.

Advanced options

The *Summary* is always worth having.

Turn off the *log* if you don't use it.

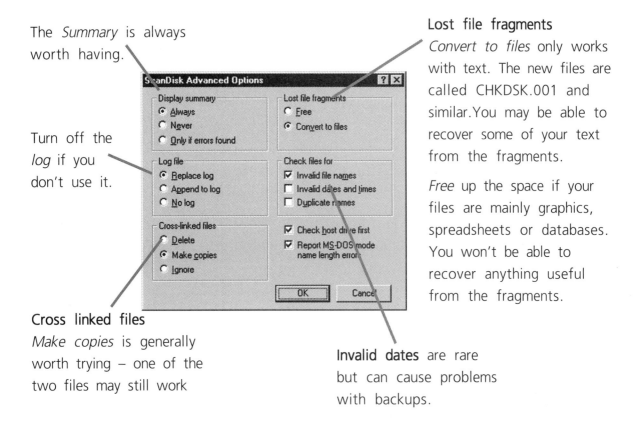

Lost file fragments

Convert to files only works with text. The new files are called CHKDSK.001 and similar.You may be able to recover some of your text from the fragments.

Free up the space if your files are mainly graphics, spreadsheets or databases. You won't be able to recover anything useful from the fragments.

Cross linked files

Make copies is generally worth trying – one of the two files may still work

Invalid dates are rare but can cause problems with backups.

Tip

If you want to know more about Scandisk, see **Hard Drives Made Simple**.

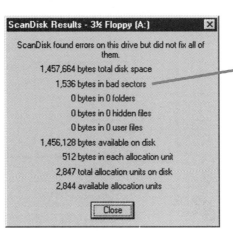

Scandisk has found bad sectors on this floppy. It has also prevented future errors by marking them off so that they are not used.

119

Backup

Modern hard disks are very reliable, but they can all develop problems eventually – some sooner than others. Making safe backup copies of your documents should be part of your regular routine.

- Do a full backup early on and after any major changes.

- Backup your document files after you have done a substantial amount of work – this may mean every day, or once a month, depending upon your activity.

With partial backups, select those folders in which you store documents and opt to backup only those which have been changed since the last backup.

For **Restore**, see
page 123

Basic steps

1 Run **Backup** from the Start menu or the disk's Properties box.

2 Do you want to **create a new backup**, add to an **existing backup** or **restore files**?

3 **Full** or **partial backup**?

4 For a *partial* backup, select the folders, and the files within them.

5 For a *full* backup, choose **All selected files**, otherwise choose **New and changed**.

6 Click 🖼 and locate the drive where the backup will be stored.

cont...

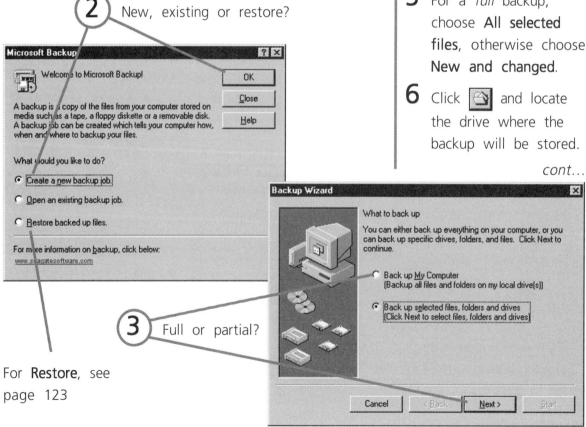

2 New, existing or restore?

3 Full or partial?

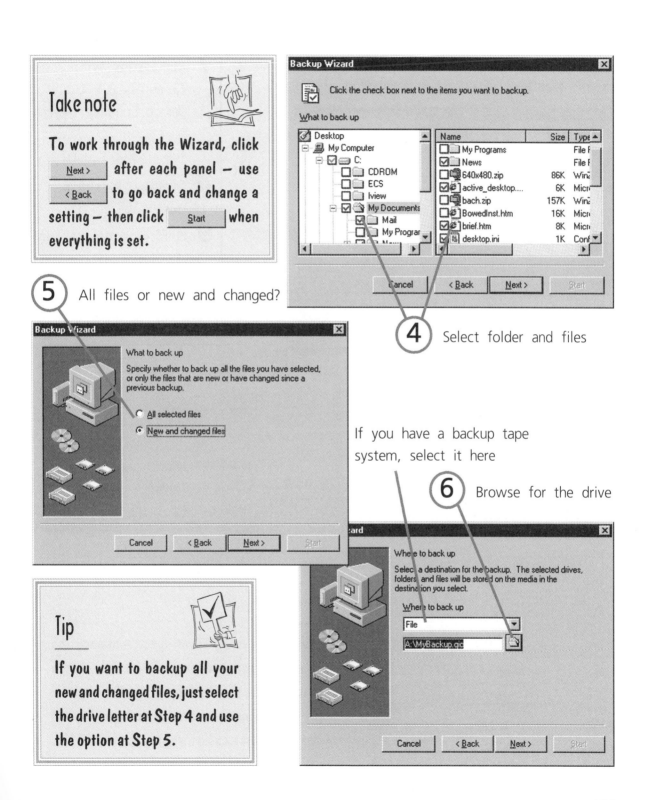

Take note

To work through the Wizard, click
Next > after each panel — use
< Back to go back and change a
setting — then click **Start** when
everything is set.

Backup Wizard

Click the check box next to the items you want to backup.

What to back up

Desktop
- My Computer
  - C:
    - CDROM
    - ECS
    - Iview
  - My Documents
    - Mail
    - My Progra...

Name	Size	Type
My Programs		File F
News		File F
640x480.zip	86K	Winz
active_desktop....	6K	Micr
bach.zip	157K	Winz
BowedInst.htm	16K	Micr
brief.htm	8K	Micr
desktop.ini	1K	Conf

Cancel   < Back   Next >   Start

⑤ All files or new and changed?

④ Select folder and files

Backup Wizard

What to back up

Specify whether to back up all the files you have selected,
or only the files that are new or have changed since a
previous backup.

○ All selected files
● New and changed files

Cancel   < Back   Next >   Start

If you have a backup tape
system, select it here

⑥ Browse for the drive

...ard

Where to back up

Select a destination for the backup. The selected drives,
folders, and files will be stored on the media in the
destination you select.

Where to back up

File

A:\MyBackup.qic

Cancel   < Back   Next >   Start

Tip

If you want to backup all your
new and changed files, just select
the drive letter at Step 4 and use
the option at Step 5.

Turn on Compare... if you have limited faith
in the quality of your backup tapes/disks

...cont

7 Make sure that
Compress is on, and
select **Compare** if you
have want to check
the backup's accuracy.

8 Give the backup a
name.

9 Finish the Wizard and
set it going.

⑦ Use compresssion

⑧ Give it a name

⑨ Set it going

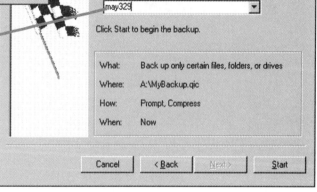

Take note

Compression usually saves space – though the
control information adds an overhead, so the
backup of a file may be larger than the original!
Some types compress more than others. Typical
savings: programs 25%; text 33%; graphics 75%.

Basic steps

1 Run **Backup** and select Restore – it should open with the **Restore** panel on top.

2 Select the file to **Restore from**.

3 Open the folders to bring the relevant ones into sight.

4 Pick the files you want to restore.

5 Click [Start].

Files are normally restored to their **Original Location**. If you want to recover old files without overwriting their new versions, restore them to a different folder.

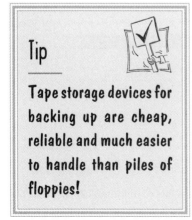

Tip

Tape storage devices for backing up are cheap, reliable and much easier to handle than piles of floppies!

With any luck, you will never have to restore a lost file. However, should you need to, it's a simple process.

① Open the Restore panel

② Select device and file

⑤ Start

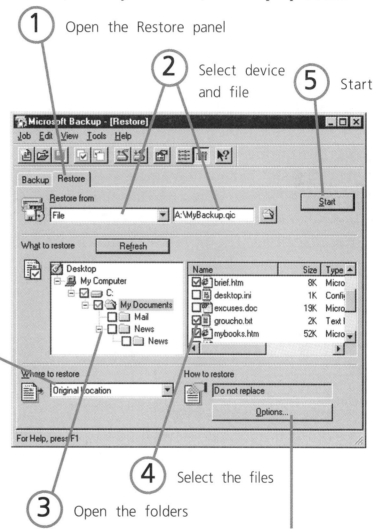

④ Select the files

③ Open the folders

If there is an existing file of the same name, Restore will not normally replace it with an old one – if you want Restore to put back an earlier version of a file, set the Options.

Disk Defragmenter

When you first start to write data onto a disk, the files go on, one after the other, with each occupying a continuous run of disk space. When you access one of these files, the drive simply finds the start point, then reads the data in a single sweep.

After the disk has been in use for some time, holes begin to appear in the layout, and not all files are stored in a continuous area. Some have been deleted, others will have grown during editing, so that they no longer fit in their original slot, but now have parts stored elsewhere on the disk. When you store a new file, there may not be a single space large enough for it, and it is stored in scattered sections. The drive is becoming *fragmented*. The data is still safe, but the access speed will suffer as the drive now has to hunt for each fragment of the file.

1 Run the **Disk Defragmenter** from the Start menu or the disk's Properties box.

2 Select the drive.

3 If you have run ScanDisk recently, click ⬚Settings...⬚ and turn off **Check for errors**.

4 Click **OK**.

5 When it starts, click ⬚Show Details⬚ to see what's going on.

6 Click ⬚Legend⬚ to find out what the symbols mean.

7 Go for a coffee – it can take up to an hour to defragment a large drive.

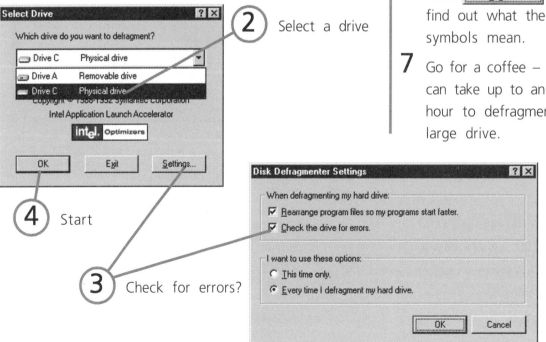

② Select a drive

④ Start

③ Check for errors?

124

(5) Show Details to see it at work

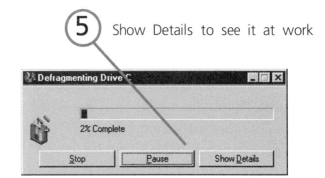

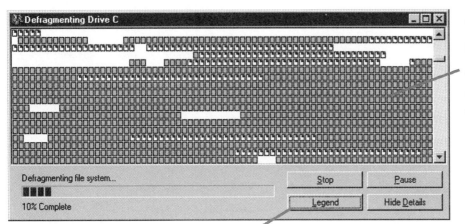

Watching the Defragmenter at work is more exciting than watching paint dry... but not much more

(6) What does it all mean?

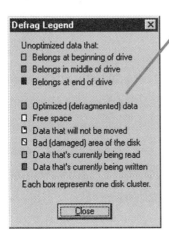

Disk Cleanup

This is a neat little utility, and well worth running regularly – especially if you spend much time on the Internet. When you are surfing the Net, your browser stores the files for the text, graphics and programs on the Web pages that you visit. This makes sense, as it means that if you go back to a page (either in the same session or at a later date), the browser can redraw it from the files, rather than having to download the whole lot again. However, if you don't revisit sites much, you can build up a lot of unwanted clutter on your disk. You can empty this cache from within your browser, but Cleanup will also do this.

The Recycle Bin can be emptied directly, or as part of the Cleanup.

Programs often create temporary files, but do not always remove them. Cleanup will tidy up after them.

1 Run **Disk Cleanup** from the Start menu.

2 After it has checked the system, the Cleanup panel opens. Select the areas to be cleaned.

3 Click **OK**.

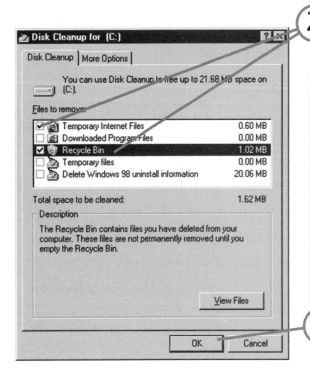

② Which files do you want to remove?

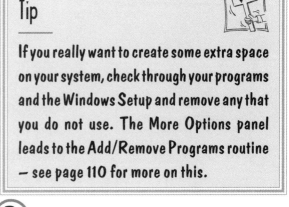

Tip

If you really want to create some extra space on your system, check through your programs and the Windows Setup and remove any that you do not use. The **More Options** panel leads to the Add/Remove Programs routine – see page 110 for more on this.

③ Click OK

Basic steps

1 Run **Windows Tune-Up** from the Start menu.

Either

2 Select **Tune up now**, click **OK** and leave it.

or

3 Select **Change my settings or schedule**, click **OK** and work through the Wizard.

4 Select the **Custom** option to set your own times.

5 Pick a time of day for the Tune-Up.

cont...

Windows Tune-Up

The Tune-Up Wizard is a simple way to run the three most important housekeeping programs – Cleanup, Scandisk and Disk Defragmenter. It can be used two ways:

● Instant tune-up – just set it going and take a break from your machine while it works

● Scheduled tasks – set it to run any or all of the chores at set, regular times.

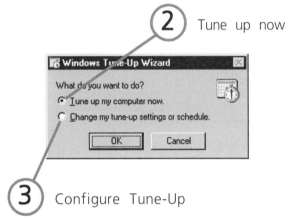

② Tune up now

③ Configure Tune-Up

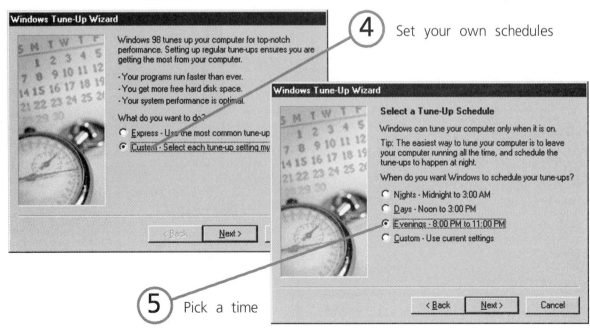

④ Set your own schedules

⑤ Pick a time

6 Click Reschedule

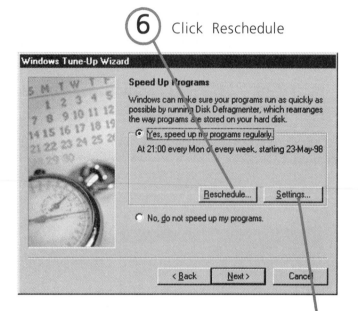

...cont

6 When you reach the **Speed Up** panel, click Reschedule... .

7 Set the time, day and frequency for the task.

8 Click Settings... .

9 Set the options for the program and click **OK**.

❏ Repeat Steps 7 and 8 for **Scandisk** and **Disk Cleanup**.

8 Click Settings

7 Set the day, time and frequency

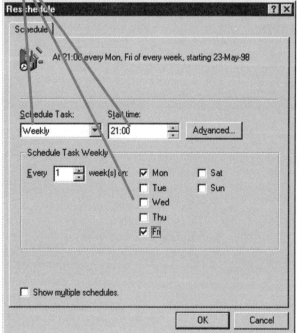

9 Set the program's options

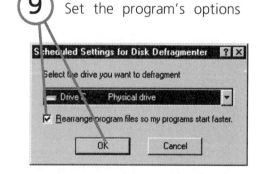

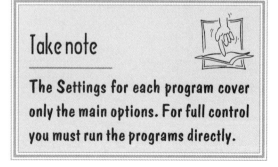

Take note

The Settings for each program cover only the main options. For full control you must run the programs directly.

Basic steps

1 Select **Scheduled Tasks** from the **System Tools** menu.

2 Right-click on a task and select **Properties**.

3 To turn a task off, clear the **Enabled** box on the **Task** panel.

4 Use the **Schedule** panel to set new times.

5 Use the **Settings** panel to adjust how the task affects your work.

Running the Tune-Up Wizard creates the set of Scheduled Tasks. You can run the Wizard again to change the schedules, but if you only want to adjust the settings of one task it is simpler to do it directly.

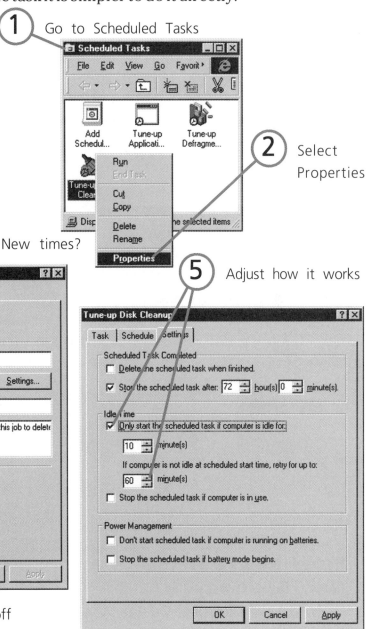

① Go to Scheduled Tasks

② Select Properties

④ New times?

⑤ Adjust how it works

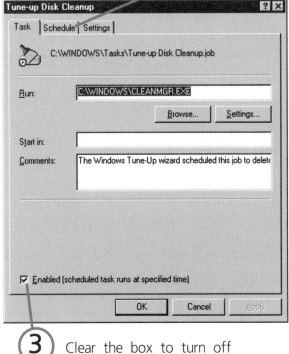

③ Clear the box to turn off

Formatting a floppy

Before you can use a new floppy disk, it must be **formatted**. This marks out magnetic tracks on the disk surface, dividing the area up into numbered blocks to provide organised storage space.

The **Format** command takes the hard work out of this – all you have to do is make sure that you know what kind of disk you are formatting.

PC disks are almost always High-Density (HD) standard – 3.5 inch, 1.44Mb capacities. You may occasionally meet a 720Kb Double-Density (DD) 3.5 inch disk.

Basic steps

1 Insert the disk into the drive.

2 Run **My Computer** or **Explorer**.

3 Right click on the A: drive and select **Format**.

4 At the dialog box, make sure that it is set for the right capacity.

5 Select **Full**.

6 Click [Start].

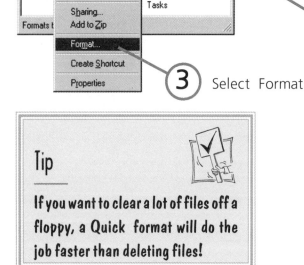

② Run My Computer

③ Select Format

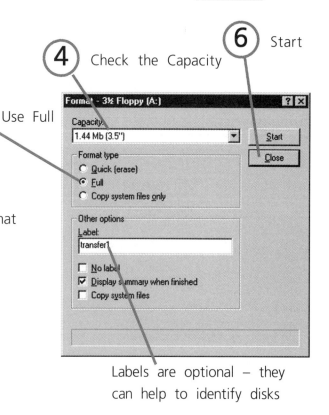

④ Check the Capacity

⑤ Use Full

⑥ Start

Labels are optional – they can help to identify disks

Tip

If you want to clear a lot of files off a floppy, a Quick format will do the job faster than deleting files!

Caring for floppies

❑ Disk drives can be mounted horizontally or vertically, but a disk will only go in one way round. If it won't fit, don't force it. Try it the other way round.

The modern 3.5 inch floppy is a far tougher beast than the older 5.25 inch ones. Its plastic casing protects it well against grime, knocks and splashes of coffee, but it still has enemies. Heat, damp and magnetism will both go through the casing and corrupt the data on the disk beneath. So, keep your disks away from radiators, sunny windowsills, magnets, heavy electrical machinery or mains cables – both produce magnetic fields.

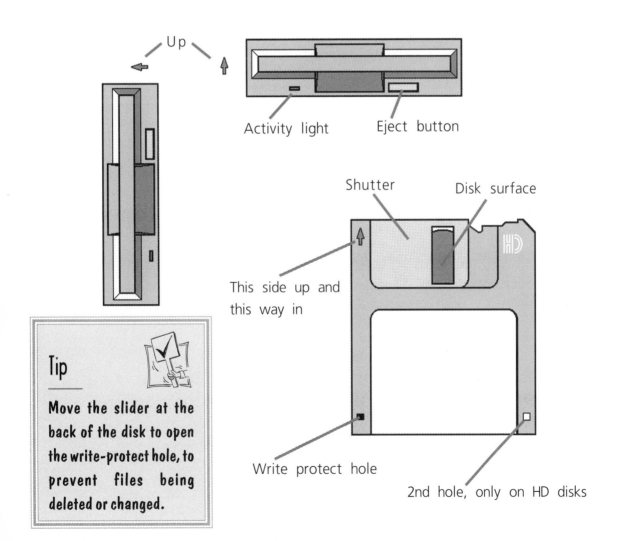

Up

Activity light   Eject button

Shutter   Disk surface

This side up and this way in

Tip

Move the slider at the back of the disk to open the write-protect hole, to prevent files being deleted or changed.

Write protect hole

2nd hole, only on HD disks

131

Summary

❏ Windows 98 is supplied with a set of very useful **system tools**.

❏ **Scandisk** can find and fix errors on your disks.

❏ **Backup** provides a simple and efficient way of creating backup copies of your files. The backups are compressed, significantly saving space.

❏ If you lose backed-up files, they can be recovered using **Restore**.

❏ The **Disk Defragmenter** should be run regularly to ensure that files are stored compactly, and can therefore be loaded faster.

❏ **Disk Cleanup** offers an easy way to find and remove unwanted files.

❏ **Windows TuneUp** will run the housekeeping jobs for you — either immediately or as **Scheduled Tasks**.

❏ Floppy disks must be fully **formatted** before they can be used.

❏ If you want to reuse a disk with old files on it, the **Quick Format** option is the fastest way to erase files.

❏ Floppies should be **stored safely** away from heat, damp and sources of magnetism.

10 Printers and accessories

Printer settings

Windows 98 knows about printers, just as it knows about most other bits of hardware that you might attach to your system. If you installed 98 over an earlier version of Windows, it will have picked up the printer settings from there. If yours was a new Windows 98 computer and you have just installed a printer (see page 136), check the settings now. Make sure that they are how you would normally want to use the printer – the settings can be changed for any special print job, using the Print Setup routine of any application program.

(see page 136)

Basic steps

1 Click **Start**.
2 Point to **Settings**.
3 Select **Printers**.
4 Right-click a printer to open its short menu.
5 Select **Properties**. Work through the panels, selecting settings to suit your normal print needs.

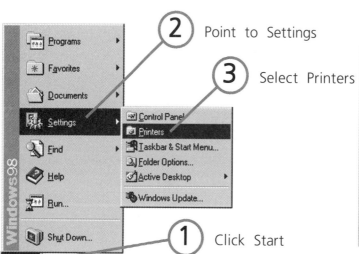

Point to Settings

Select Printers

Click Start

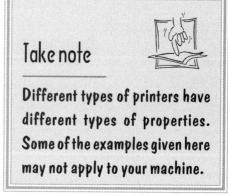

Take note

Different types of printers have different types of properties. Some of the examples given here may not apply to your machine.

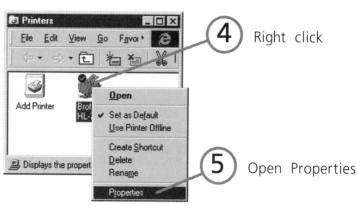

Right click

Open Properties

Tip

The Fax is also a 'printer'. Paper size, greyscales and other 'printing' aspects are controlled from here.

All printers have a **Paper** panel, with **Paper Size** and **Orientation** options. Alternative **Layouts** are normally only found on Postscript printers

If your printer can work at different **resolutions**, remember that the higher the resolution, the slower the printing – and the more ink/ toner it uses.

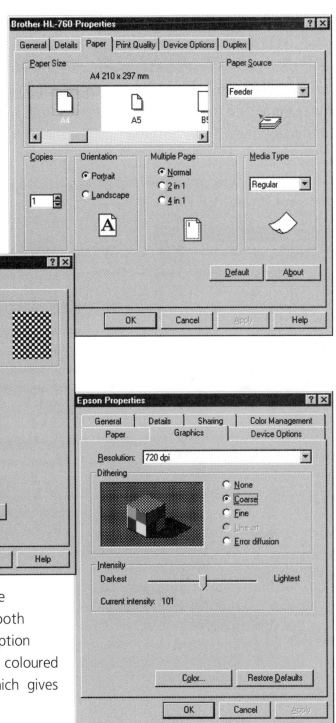

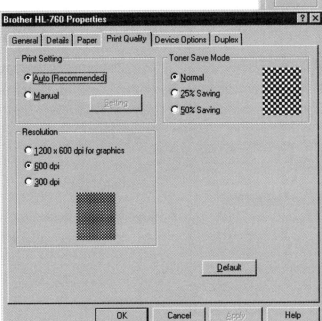

On the **Graphics** panel, you may have **Dithering** options. Dithering can smooth curves and angled lines. Test each option with a page containing a mixture of coloured bitmaps and line drawings to see which gives best results on your printer.

Adding a printer

Windows 98 has drivers for all major – and many minor – printers in existence at the time of its design. (Drivers are programs that convert the formatting information from a word-processor or other application into the right codes for the printer.) If you have a *very* new machine, you should use the drivers on the setup disk that came with it.

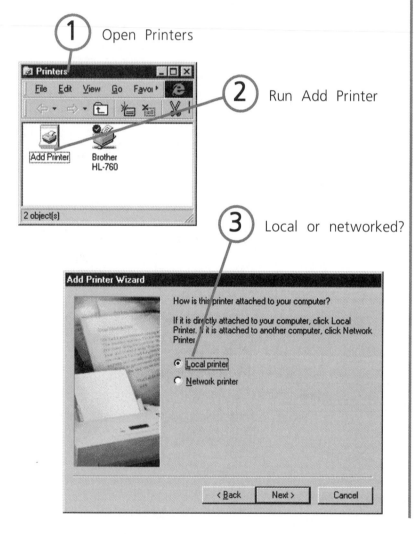

① Open Printers

② Run Add Printer

③ Local or networked?

Basic steps

1 Open the **Printers** folder.

2 Run **Add Printer.**

3 If you are on a network, select **Local** (attached to your PC) or **Network** printer.

Either

4 Pick the **Manufacturer** then the **Printer** from the lists.

or

5 Insert a disk with the printer driver and click **Have Disk.**

6 Select the **Port** – normally LPT1.

7 Change the name if you like – networked printers are often given nicknames to identify them.

8 Set this as **the default** if appropriate.

9 At the final stage opt for the test print then click **Finish** and wait.

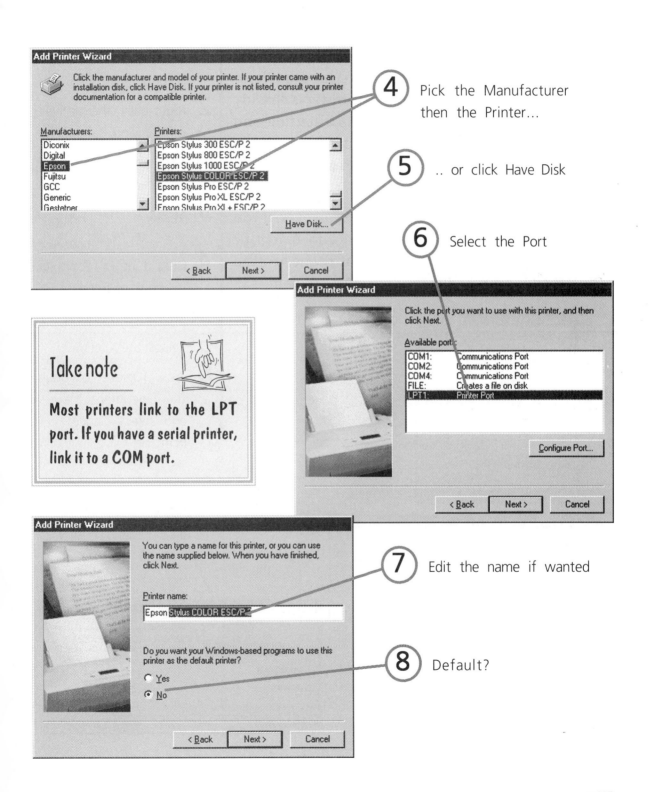

Add Printer Wizard

Click the manufacturer and model of your printer. If your printer came with an installation disk, click Have Disk. If your printer is not listed, consult your printer documentation for a compatible printer.

Manufacturers:
- Diconix
- Digital
- **Epson**
- Fujitsu
- GCC
- Generic
- Gestetner

Printers:
- Epson Stylus 300 ESC/P 2
- Epson Stylus 800 ESC/P 2
- Epson Stylus 1000 ESC/P 2
- **Epson Stylus COLOR ESC/P 2**
- Epson Stylus Pro ESC/P 2
- Epson Stylus Pro XL ESC/P 2
- Epson Stylus Pro XL + ESC/P 2

Have Disk...

< Back   Next >   Cancel

④ Pick the Manufacturer then the Printer...

⑤ .. or click Have Disk

⑥ Select the Port

Add Printer Wizard

Click the port you want to use with this printer, and then click Next.

Available ports:

COM1:	Communications Port
COM2:	Communications Port
COM4:	Communications Port
FILE:	Creates a file on disk
LPT1:	Printer Port

Configure Port...

< Back   Next >   Cancel

Take note

Most printers link to the LPT port. If you have a serial printer, link it to a COM port.

Add Printer Wizard

You can type a name for this printer, or you can use the name supplied below. When you have finished, click Next.

Printer name:

Epson Stylus COLOR ESC/P 2

Do you want your Windows-based programs to use this printer as the default printer?

○ Yes
● No

< Back   Next >   Cancel

⑦ Edit the name if wanted

⑧ Default?

Managing the queue

When you send a document for printing, Windows 98 will happily handle it in the background. It prepares the file for the printer, stores it in a queue if the printer is already busy or off-line, pushes the pages out one at a time and deletes the temporary files it has created. Nothing visible happens on screen – unless the printer runs out of paper or has other faults.

This is fine when things run smoothly. However, if you decide you want to cancel the printing of a document, or have sent several and want to push one to the head of the queue, then you do need to see things. No problem!

Basic steps

1 Open the **Printers** folder.

2 Right-click the active printer and select **Open** from its menu.

❏ **To change the order**

3 Select the file you want to move.

4 Drag it up or down to its new position.

❏ **To cancel printing**

5 Select the file(s).

6 Press [**Delete**] or open the **Document** menu and select **Cancel Printing**.

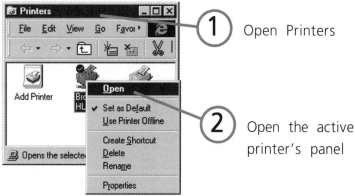

(1) Open Printers

(2) Open the active printer's panel

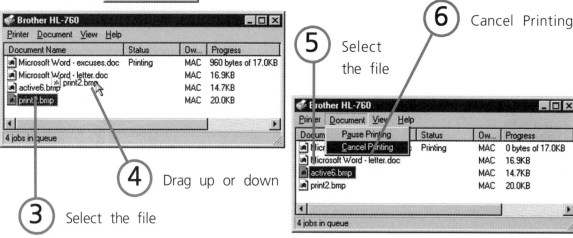

(5) Select the file

(6) Cancel Printing

(4) Drag up or down

(3) Select the file

138

Basic steps

1 Open the **Printers** folder.

2 Open the folder containing the document file to be printed.

3 Arrange the windows so that you can see both clearly.

4 Drag the file across and drop it on the printer icon.

❑ Windows 98 will print simple text files instantly, for others it will open the related application, print from there then close the application.

Direct printing

You do not necessarily have to load a document into an application to print it. Windows 95 can print many types of documents directly from the files.

Bitmapped graphics (.BMP files), plain text and the documents from any Microsoft Office application can be printed in this way, as can those from other newer software.

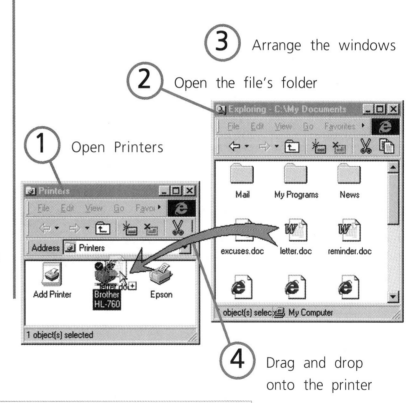

③ Arrange the windows

② Open the file's folder

① Open Printers

④ Drag and drop onto the printer

Take note

You can use this method to print on machines that are not connected to your PC. Simply store the document file on floppy and drag it onto the printer icon on the PC attached to the printer you want to use.

The Clipboard

The Clipboard is a mechanism for copying and moving text, graphics, files, folders and other types of data within and between applications. Whatever you are doing in Windows, it is always at hand and used in the same way.

Any Windows application that handles data in any form has an Edit menu. This always contains three core options – Cut, Copy and Paste – plus varying others. You can see these on the two Edit menus shown below.

- **Cut** removes a selected block of text or object, and transfers it to the Clipboard's memory.

- **Copy** takes a copy of the selected item into the Clipboard, but without removing it.

- **Paste** copies whatever is in the Clipboard into the current cursor position in the application.

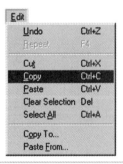

The Edit menus from Paint (left) and WordPad (below). The core options are always there.

Basic steps

❑ **To Cut**

1 Select the text or object.

2 Open the **Edit** menu.

3 Click **Cut**.

❑ **To Copy**

1 Select the text or object.

2 Open the **Edit** menu.

3 Click **Copy**.

❑ **To Paste from the Clipboard**

1 Place the cursor at the point where you want the selected item to be inserted.

2 Open the **Edit** menu.

3 Click **Paste**.

Take note

Cut and Copy are only available after you have selected something. Paste is only available if there is something in the Clipboard.

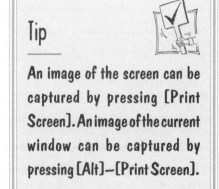

Tip

An image of the screen can be captured by pressing [Print Screen]. An image of the current window can be captured by pressing [Alt]–[Print Screen].

Basic steps

To select text

1 Place the text cursor at the start of the block.

2 Drag the pointer to spread a highlight over the block.

3 You are ready to Cut or Copy.

To select one object

1 Click on it to get handles around its edges.

To select a set of adjacent objects

1 Imagine a rectangle that will enclose all the objects.

2 Place the pointer at one corner of this rectangle.

3 Drag the broken outline to enclose them all.

4 Release the mouse button and check that all have acquired handles.

Selecting for Cut and Copy

These techniques work with most Windows applications. Some will also offer additional selection methods of their own, which may be more convenient in some situations.

You normally select **text** by dragging the pointer over the desired block of characters.

The highlight shows the selected text.

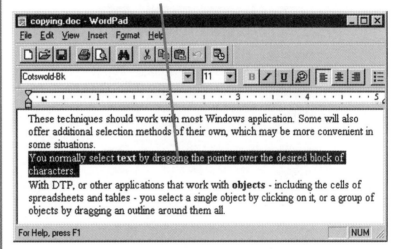

With DTP, or other applications that work with **objects** – including the cells of spreadsheets and tables – you select a single object by clicking on it, or a group of objects by dragging an outline around them all.

The enclosing outline

Selected objects are usually indicated by handles.

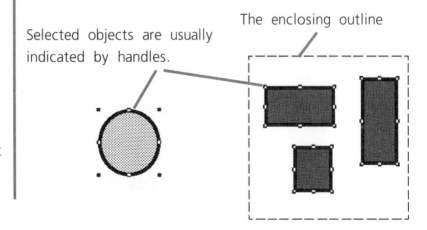

MS-DOS programs

Some DOS programs can be run directly from within Windows 98, simply by adding them to the Start menu. Set them to run in a Window, rather than Full Screen, to gives you access to the Edit facilities. The number of screen lines and the font can be adjusted to suit yourself.

Basic steps

- ☐ Setting up
1 Open the **Properties** dialog box for the program's shortcut.
2 Switch to the **Screen** panel.
3 Check that the **Usage** is set to **Window**.
4 Set the **Initial size**.

2 Open the Screen panel

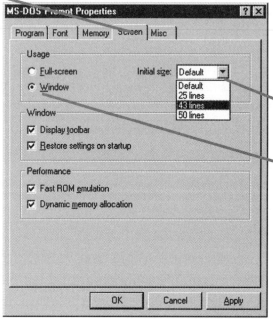

4 Set the Size

3 Run in a window

Turn on the Toolbar in DOS windows for easy editing and font control.

The MS-DOS Prompt

This gives you the standard DOS C:> prompt. Use it for those programs that will not run from a shortcut, or that are rarely used.

Make sure the MS-DOS Prompt is set to run in a window.

Copy and Paste in MS-DOS

❑ Copying

1 Open the **Control** menu.

2 Select **Edit**, then **Mark**.

3 Highlight the text you want to copy.

4 Open the Control menu again and select **Edit – Copy.**

5 Switch to your target application and paste the text there.

There is an Edit item in the Control menu in DOS windows, and a set of Toolbar icons that can be used to copy text between DOS and Windows applications. Pasting is the same as normal, but to copy you must first use **Edit – Mark** to highlight the block of text. To do this, imagine a rectangle that encloses the text. Point to one corner and drag the highlight to the opposite corner.

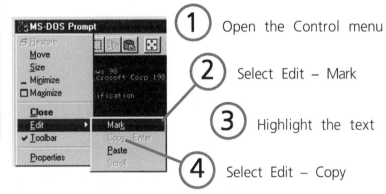

① Open the Control menu

② Select Edit – Mark

③ Highlight the text

④ Select Edit – Copy

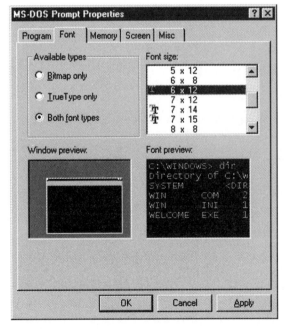

Fonts

The **A** icon on the Toolbar takes you to the Font property panel of the MS-DOS window. Note that the window's size varies with the font size, so that it holds the same quantity of text. The **Window Preview** shows the size of the window relative to the whole screen.

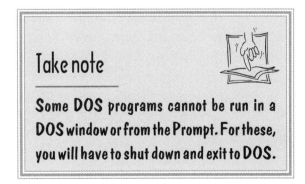

Take note

Some DOS programs cannot be run in a **DOS** window or from the Prompt. For these, you will have to shut down and exit to DOS.

CD Player

Your CD-ROM drive is not just for installation disks or multimedia software. It can also play audio CDs. Put one in the drive and Windows 98 will play it automatically. The standard Play, Stop, Fast Forward and Rewind controls are there, plus extra ones for scheduling play.

Basic steps

❑ **Choosing tracks**

1 From the **Disc** menu, select **Edit Play List**.

2 Select an unwanted track and click Remove ->.

3 Click OK.

❑ **Play order**

4 Open the **Options** menu and select a play order.

❑ **Volume control**

5 Click on the speaker icon and adjust the slider on the **Volume** panel.

or

6 Turn on **Mute** for instant silence.

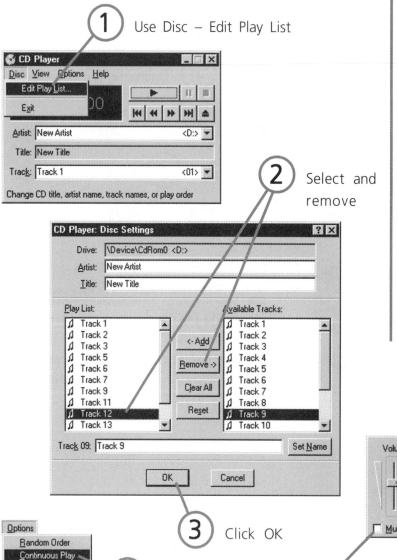

(1) Use Disc – Edit Play List

(2) Select and remove

(3) Click OK

(4) Select a play order

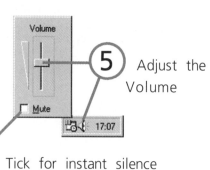

(5) Adjust the Volume

(6) Tick for instant silence

144

Basic steps

Character Map

The Character Map

1 Go to the **Accessories** menu and select **Character Map**.

2 Select the **Font**.

3 Click on a character to highlight it.

4 Click [Select] to place it into **Characters to Copy**.

5 Go back over Steps 3 and 4 as necessary.

6 Click [Copy] to copy to the Clipboard.

7 Return to your application and **Paste** the characters into it.

This shows the full set of characters that are present in any given font, and allows you to select one or more individual characters for copying into other applications. Its main use is probably for picking up Wingdings for decoration, or the odd foreign letter or mathematical symbols in otherwise straight text.

The characters are rather small, but you can get a better look at a character, by holding the mouse button down while you point at it. This produces an enlarged image.

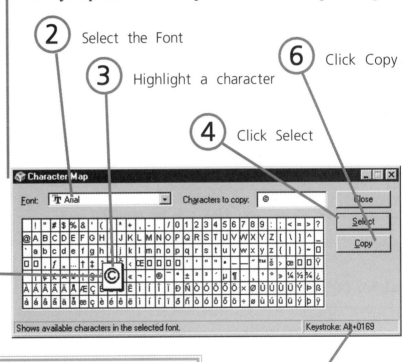

② Select the Font

③ Highlight a character

⑥ Click Copy

④ Click Select

Hold down the button to magnify

Note the keystroke

Tip

If you are going to use a character often, learn its keystroke. This is shown at the bottom right. For Alt+ ones, hold [Alt] and type the number on the Number Pad.

145

Summary

❑ Printer settings can be adjusted if wanted. The **Paper** and **resolution** options should be checked.

❑ **Adding a new printer** is easy. Windows 98 has drivers for almost all printers, though you may need a manufacturer's disk with very new models.

❑ Printing is handled in the **background**, so that – apart from slowing things up a bit – it does not interfere with your other work.

❑ Files are stored in a **queue** before printing. You can change their order or delete them if necessary.

❑ You can **print** a document **directly** by dragging the file to the printer icon.

❑ The **Clipboard** is used for copying text and graphics within and between programs, and for copying files and folders across disks and folders.

❑ **Text can be selected** by dragging a highlight over it.

❑ Individual **images and files can be selected** by clicking on them. Groups of objects can be selected by dragging outlines around them.

❑ **MS-DOS programs** can be run directly from shortcuts, or through the MS-DOS prompt. In either case, they should be set to run in a window, not full screen, to get access to the cut and paste facilities.

❑ CD Player will play **audio CDs**.

❑ The **Character map** allows you to select special characters from a selected font, to paste into an application.

Index